NEAR THE CROSS

NEAR THE CROSS

A Lenten Journey of Prayer

KENNETH H. CARTER, JR.

Abingdon Press / Nashville

NEAR THE CROSS
A Lenten Journey of Prayer
BY KENNETH H. CARTER, JR.
Copyright © 2015 by Abingdon Press
All rights reserved.

Scripture quotations in this publication, unless otherwise indicated, are from the Common English Bible, © Copyright 2011 by Common English Bible, and are used by permission.

Scripture quotations noted NRSV are taken from the New Revised Standard Version of the Bible, copyright 1989, Division of Christian Education of the National Council of the Churches of Christ in the United States of America. Used by permission. All rights reserved.

ISBN-13: 9781501800917

15 16 17 18 19 20 21 22 23 24—10 9 8 7 6 5 4 3 2 1

Manufactured in the United States of America

Contents

Introduction

In Lent, we begin a journey that leads us to the cross, where we encounter a person, Jesus Christ. In this time of renewed focus on our spiritual lives, prayer stands front and center. It is through prayer that we come to know and imitate the mind of Christ. Prayer will be our guide over the next forty days. Each week, we will explore a different aspect of the cross and the Christian life, and we will discover how prayer draws us near the cross and into the heart of Jesus. It is my hope that you will grow in your faith as you read and pray throughout the season of Lent. I am grateful to share this journey with you.

We are accompanied on our journey by a brief and profound resource: Paul's Letter to the Philippians. On the surface, the occasion of the letter is Paul's gratitude for a gift they have sent in support of his mission. But just beneath the surface are clues to other important matters of life and faith. I am an ordinary Christian who has been given extraordinary opportunities to serve in the church and beyond. On the surface, I write in order to encourage Christians, as individuals and in small groups, to grow more deeply in the faith. But just beneath the surface, I find significant help and hope in the words of the apostle Paul.

When Paul writes about his partnership in the gospel with the Philippians, I see the impossibility of living the Christian life in isolation from others. I recognize the destructiveness of attempting to be a solo leader. When Paul speaks of the work that God has only just begun in us, I am encouraged to take the next step in my faith and trust the outcome to God. When Paul points to the image of the crucified and risen Christ, I am given a new and higher model for unity through service. When Paul speaks of his contentment regardless of abundance or scarcity, I trust in the capacity of God to provide in all circumstances.

Just beneath the surface in this extraordinary letter, there is help and hope for individuals, congregations, and denominations. Apart from the gifts of others, an individual's spiritual journey is not sustainable. Apart from the imitation of Christ, our life together as congregations will disintegrate into a collision of personal preferences. And apart from a commitment to the unity of the church, with Jesus Christ as Lord and Savior, our denominations will degenerate into an assembly of competing voices seeking power and control.

The season of Lent is an intentional time of purgation, as we set aside our private and collective agendas in order to focus on the example of Jesus. This will inevitably be the way of the cross for us—the road of suffering and conflict—on the way to resurrection and new life. It may be that you come to this book and this season with a particular struggle weighing upon you: disappointment, disillusionment, division, or some other difficult matter. The themes of this work can be helpful to you: perseverance, unity, reconciliation, joy, gratitude. By praying and focusing on Paul's words to the Philippians, you can receive encouragement, find strength, and hear God's call to grow closer to Jesus.

I have served as a pastor, a district superintendent, and a bishop in The United Methodist Church. In the local church, I loved the weekly practice of teaching and preaching from the Scriptures. In the apostle Paul, I found a mentor and brother who knew the flaws and faithfulness of congregations; indeed, he could confess his own flawed past and his aspiration to be faithful! In the ministry of supervision (as a district superintendent and bishop), I have benefited from Paul's more expansive vision: He no longer leads a congregation week by week, but he speaks at a distance from a perspective of loving objectivity. The distance gives him a perspective that helps him to take the longview, from this life into the life to come.

Yet Paul writes not only or chiefly to religious professionals. He is most helpful reflecting with ordinary women and men who are seeking to make sense of life and faith. His is a profound Christian spirituality. It incorporates our need for one another, our calling to be servants, God's desire for unity in the church, the ongoing process of discipleship and formation, the power of narrative and testimony, the need for resilience and perseverance, and the experience of gratitude and fulfillment. Each chapter of this book focuses on one of these themes, demonstrating Paul's insights in the Book of Philippians and how prayer can help us make these insights into a way of life. So much of what passes for Christian spirituality in our time can be individualist or escapist. It often trends toward personal preferences that are enclosed within particular sectors of the church. It aims for the quick fix and insists on immediate transformation. And it relies more on our own efforts and skills than the gifts of God. Here, a brief New Testament letter is a needed corrective for a church that often looks more like a corporate institution than an organic body. Prayer is also needed to help us hear God's voice rather than the echoes of our own opinions.

My prayer for you, in the season of Lent, is that you will find help and hope in the Letter to the Philippians, in this collection of reflections on Paul's words, and in your own life of prayer. Paul's words can assist us in reframing many of the questions we have in the spiritual journey. I find his encouragement to be an amazing gift from God in a season of despair and discouragement. And I find his challenge to be a prophetic admonition from God in a culture of cynicism and complacency.

May these words, through the inspiration of the Holy Spirit, shape us over the forty days of Lent. And may they guide us more deeply into Christian community, which is always located near the cross.

Partnership, Community, and the Cross

Scripture: Read Philippians 1:1-30

"I'm glad because of the way you have been my partners in the ministry of the gospel . . ." (Philippians 1:5)

On a number of occasions I have traveled to Africa to witness, encourage, and learn from leaders in God's mission there. On one wall in the Johannesburg Airport there is an African proverb:

"If you want to travel fast, walk alone.
If you want to travel far, walk together."

This proverb summarizes an important aspect of our Christian life, which we see from the very first verses of the Book of Philippians: The Christian life is life in community. The apostle Paul is remembered for his strategic role as a missionary in the early Christian movement. He is regarded as a singularly important leader, theologian, and apostle. And yet Paul was not a lone ranger. He writes in Philippians 1:5: "I'm glad because of the way you have been my partners in the ministry of the gospel." Paul thanks God for the Christians in Philippi because he recognizes that they are his partners; he could not have done his work of ministry without them.

We were not created to be alone. We flourish in community. Other words in our theological vocabulary help us to carry the full weight and importance of what this means for our faith: sharing, partnership, and fellowship come to mind. But community is foundational. Whatever else the church is, we are first of all a community. And as followers of Jesus we feel a sense of community because we share in a mission: the ministry of the gospel. Aspects of that mission might be . . .

- to raise our children to live out the values of Jesus;
- to share our resources with the poor;
- to help persons outside the church to overcome barriers that separate them from God;
- to offer sanctuary where persons can experience God in the midst of busy lives;
- to help lonely people find connections;
- to help wounded people find healing;
- to help condemned people find grace.

We might all focus on different dimensions of our collective mission, but in doing so we are all partners in the ministry of the gospel.

In Lent as we journey toward the cross of Jesus, we reflect more deeply on the grace of God. It's important to remember that Paul wrote the Letter to the Philippians while he was in prison because of Christ. I'm sure Paul thought again and again about God's grace, which sustained him in captivity and enabled the gospel to spread through others while he was in prison (Philippians 1:12-18). The Philippians too are "partners in God's grace,"

Paul writes, even in his imprisonment (Philippians 1:7). When Paul speaks of partnership, he uses the Greek word *koinonia*, which has the sense of a close mutual relationship (Philippians 1:5). This word describes the deep spiritual connection among the believers in the Book of Acts (2:42), and elsewhere in the New Testament it refers to the church's connection with Jesus (1 Corinthians 1:9). The community Paul envisions is one that includes the Philippians, himself, and the God who meets him through Jesus Christ, the embodiment of grace. This is a compelling image: In a context of isolation, separation, and loneliness, Paul imagines a rich and full community, one for which he gives prayerful thanks (1:3). The Philippians are partners with Paul in the gospel. They are more than a human community; they share a mystical communion.

From the perspective of history and eternity, Paul traveled far, not fast. His influence has spanned generations. His intellect has inspired reformations. His traveling companions were sometimes individuals and sometimes communities of disciples. But it is clear that his leadership and ministry take a communal shape.

The Connected, Collaborative Leader

In my early years as a minister, my image of ministry was very much influenced by what some have described as the heroic solo leader. I sat in the pew and listened to a compelling preacher. I sat in a classroom and learned from a wise professor. I imagined that my calling was to somehow carry on that work; I would be an inspiring preacher, taking what I had heard in the solitude of a pastor's study and sharing it with a congregation, or poring over texts in preparation for writing scholarly articles and books and lecturing to students.

These are honorable activities. But across three decades, I have discovered ministry to be a very different vocation. The actual work is less static and more dynamic than I had imagined. It cannot easily be located in a particular space, namely the defined offices of a professional. And at times, if I am honest, it has not always been clear who was the teacher and who was the student!

It is no secret among professional ministers that there is a high risk of burnout. It is a spiritually taxing career. But I am convinced that much of this burnout in North American culture is due to a distorted image of ministry. The heroic solo leader discovers, over time, that human needs are vast and complex. The heroic solo leader learns, over time, that he or she lacks the capacity to change people. Only God has the power to change, heal, and save. In the Scriptures, salvation history takes the longview. And in the Scriptures, salvation is a corporate activity.

If you want to travel fast, walk alone. If you want to travel far, walk together.

To walk together is to be in partnership. In partnership we rejoice with those who rejoice and weep with those who weep (Romans 12:15). The alternative to the heroic solo leader is the one who knows she is at her best when she is attentive to the presence of others. The gifts, strengths, and prayers of others uphold the connected, collaborative leader.

Heroic solo leadership is not sustainable. Connected and collaborative leadership is sustainable. Heroic solo leadership is fast and efficient. Connected and collaborative leadership is shared and steady. For this reason the cross is at the center of the community, which carries it together. We are all called to take up the cross, but God calls none of us to take it up alone. We bear one another's burdens.

For many years, our family participated in a walk to alleviate hunger, at both local and global levels. When we began, my wife and I undertook the ten-mile walk as a couple. After our children were born, we carried them or pushed them in strollers. They gradually began to walk portions of the route, and in time they outpaced us. The impact of this shared family experience did not occur to me until one of our daughters gave a mission witness in our congregation. She recalled her fifteen-year journey related to this particular hunger walk: First she was carried; then she began to walk; then she inspired others to walk. We had indeed made this journey together.

It occurs to me that this experience echoes the wisdom found in Paul's letter to his friends in Philippi. They are his partners in the gospel. He gives them words of encouragement and instruction from prison, and they in turn lift him up by their support. Paul carries or inspires them when it's necessary; they carry or inspire him when circumstances are different. Paul is mature enough to have learned that he is not a solo heroic leader. He has learned to walk not fast, but far in his faithful pilgrimage.

Developing Community

Community and partnership in the gospel is a developmental process. Such partnership is a grace of God, and it is God's gift to us that we grow in this grace. Community is never static; we grow more deeply in relationship to one another, or we grow apart. Growing closer is often the result of a set of intentional practices: praying and singing together, confessing our sins and asking forgiveness, serving alongside one another, telling our stories and listening to the lives of others. Individuals grow and mature; this is also true for communities.

Years ago I participated in training in the area of group process and community formation. Four stages of group process were identified: *inclusion, shared experience, trust,* and *task*. Inclusion is about being welcomed into a community. Here a potential member of the community is asking a very basic question: Will I be included in this group? Many congregations ignore the need for resolution to this important question. I cannot fully focus on the mission, doctrine, or traditions of a local community if I am unsure about whether I am invited to participate fully within it.

Shared experience is the journey of coming to know other people in ordinary life. It is passing through the seasons of our lives together. Here we acknowledge that this stage cannot be accelerated. It simply takes time to get to know each other. The realities of mobility and migration disrupt shared experience; whenever we are uprooted and enter a new community, the process must start over. And so we begin anew in the stage of shared experience, celebrating major events and holidays, noticing small changes, paying attention to rhythms of daily life. Only through deep and sustained shared experience do communities move to trust.

Trust is a deeper relationship of vulnerability, in which we become more transparent to each other. When conversations are superficial and trivial, it is a sign that we are not in a place of trust. When we are sharing deeply and personally, trust is present. In the first chapter of Philippians, Paul reflects on the very intense matter of life and death:

> I hope with daring courage that Christ's greatness will be seen in my body, now as always, whether I live or die. Because for me, living serves Christ and dying is even better. If I continue to live in this world, I get results from my work. But I don't know what I prefer. I'm torn between the two because I want to leave this

life and be with Christ, which is far better. However, it's more important for me to stay in this world for your sake. I'm sure of this: I will stay alive and remain with all of you to help your progress and the joy of your faith, and to increase your pride in Christ Jesus through my presence when I visit you again.

(Philippians 1:20-26)

In this meditation of a profound question—whether Paul will live or die, and what that means—the apostle displays a profound trust in the community to which he writes. As a pastor I have listened to men and women reflect on their lives, and in the face of death I have at times been a witness to extraordinary faith and trust. In these moments two realizations have come to me: I have been the recipient of a deep trust, and I have been standing on holy ground.

Once we have moved through the stages of inclusion, shared experience, and trust, we are prepared to engage fully in the task, or the mission. We often err in racing too quickly to the mission, the action, and the agenda. Without inclusion, shared experience, and trust, we have a fragile foundation upon which to undertake the mission. Paul's apostolic ministry was grounded in deeply communal relationships that were nurtured over time. Because of this, he could rightly say that the Philippians were his partners in the gospel.

As Paul writes, he always keeps the centrality of the mission before himself and us. The participation of the Philippians in Paul's mission included a significant financial investment; the occasion of the letter is the gratitude Paul has for the gift he has received from them. It is true that persons draw close to each other in order to fulfill a mission, and that being in mission together deepens relationships.

Many Christians have had the experience of participation in mission teams, whether in an impoverished rural community

17

or urban neighborhood, in their own country of origin or after traveling a great distance. While the mission is often clear—to alleviate hunger, to offer medical care, to share the gospel—a byproduct can be a profound fellowship and depth of relationship with their fellow workers and the communities they serve. Such a relationship emerges and deepens over time if it continues to be nourished. A spiritual director once commented to me that fellowship is never our goal or aim; fellowship is the gift that God gives to us when we are in mission and service together!

This process of community formation is the good work that God has begun in us, which Paul mentions to the Philippians in verse 6. For years as a pastor, I would come alongside young people who were preparing to be confirmed in the church. This included study, mentoring, service, prayer, and learning about the church. In conversations prior to the confirmation service, we would reflect together on two essential facets of discipleship: making a profession of faith in Jesus Christ and becoming a member of his body, the church. Formation in faith is the good work that God has begun in us, and, humanly speaking, it is never completed or finished. Yet it always takes place alongside our fellow disciples.

Paul's spiritual practice of community is a profoundly significant one for us. In our seasons of loneliness, isolation, and separation, he is our model. He reminds us that, as members of the body of Christ, we are never alone. Authentic fellowship (koinonia) is far from a superficial experience of chatting in a church fellowship hall; it is the life-giving reality that sustains us in every season of life, whether that be mourning or dancing, absence or presence, distance or nearness.

Prayer and Community: I Keep You In My Heart

Paul says of the Philippians, "I keep you in my heart" (1:7). A deeper spiritual engagement with Lent and with a letter like this one moves us into a more profound experience of Christian community. I am reminded of friends who were crucial to my own spiritual journey in each local church that I served. One was a building supply salesman with little formal education. Another was a fundraiser who gave two years in retirement to full-time service in our congregation. Yet another was a gracious and gregarious woman who sought out those in a large church who were new to the community and helped them to transition from strangers to friends. I think also of brothers and sisters across the global church: a physician in Haiti; a businesswoman and seminarian in Russia; an evangelist in England; a colleague bishop in Cuba; a missionary couple in Bolivia; a pastor friend from another denomination in Maine.

Our prayer life strengthens this experience of Christian community. Paul gives thanks for the Philippian church every time he prays (Philippians 1:3-4). He offers his own prayers for them, asking God to make their love rich with knowledge and insight and to fill them with righteousness (1:9-11). Think about those in your own community. How do you pray for them? How can prayer strengthen the connection and partnership that you have with them? Through our prayers we become mindful of the needs of others, and through others' prayers on our behalf we become aware of their care and concern for us. Think also about those who are far away, but who remain connected to you. Praying for them is an important way for you to keep them in your heart, as Paul does with the Philippians (1:7).

As disciples of Jesus, we pattern our lives after his. Jesus makes a place in his life for all kinds of persons—lepers, children, women, the poor, the persecuted, the sick, and the hungry. As we read in the Gospels, he is moved with compassion to make space in his life for those in his inner circle (Peter, James, and John) and those he encounters in his daily life. As his disciples, we are challenged to imitate his life. We are compassionate toward those near to us, and we include those whose paths intersect with ours. Part of this means loving them in tangible, physical ways. And part of it means turning our prayer life outward, praying with others and for others, and asking them to pray for us in turn.

In this way our hearts, over time, are enlarged. We make space in our lives, and in our prayers, for friends, strangers, and enemies. We extend our acts of compassion to an increasingly large and diverse assembly of brothers and sisters. We begin to envision the banquet table of God's grace as one that brings together all kinds of people, and we discover that many of them do not resemble us at all!

Christian community is much deeper than a collection of like-minded, homogeneous persons. Authentic community challenges our assumptions and stereotypes about one another. It binds us in relationship with brothers and sisters who are brought together for the sole reason that we share the name of Jesus Christ; it brings us together because we have all become participants and coworkers in his mission. The early Christian movement broke down barriers of race and ethnicity, and it moved beyond boundaries of nation and tribe. This was a movement of the Holy Spirit, and the fruit of this movement was redefined relationship, grounded not in biology or family but faith and grace.

The enlarging of our hearts can lead us to a rich and imaginative fellowship that is always near to us. Two of my favorite Sundays each year in worship are World Communion and All Saints. World Communion Sunday reminds us that the church has always transcended our definition of national and political borders. Indeed, the body of Christ is global in its truest expression! And All Saints Sunday keeps before us the reality that we are in community with those who have entered eternal life. Those who have died, all the way back to the time of the apostles and before, are and always will be our sisters and brothers in Christ.

Thus the church of Jesus Christ transcends our usual conceptions of space (World Communion) and time (All Saints) as we sing "In Christ There Is No East or West" and "For All the Saints." The poverty of our spiritual lives is often due to a flattening of our liturgical practice. If we neglect such occasions in worship, we miss opportunities to recognize and celebrate the great gift of our life together in Christ. In contrast, when we affirm these connections in prayer and worship, we experience the abundance of God's provision. We are baptized into a fellowship of believers that is greater than we often imagine!

One of my mentors would often use a phrase about significant people in his life, saying that "these women and men have been church for me!" I think he was naming the particular encouragers, supporters, and advocates who had made spaces in their own lives to offer Christ to him. And at the same time, these men and women were never far from his heart; he would tell their stories, celebrate their gifts, give thanks for their presence in his own life, and yes, pray for them!

To say the words *I keep you in my heart* is to be prayerfully reminded that we are not alone. It is most often the case that

I am not physically present with many of those friends and mentors who have shaped my life and faith. Indeed, in Paul's words, some have left this life and now live with Christ (1:23). And yet, when I am conscious of a spiritual reality, I realize that I am always in the presence of a rich Christian community, regardless of where I am or what I am about on a given day. And this is the grace of God.

Questions for Reflection and Discussion

1. When have you been tempted to travel fast and walk alone? Why?

2. Can you recall an experience when you walked together and traveled far? Who were your fellow travelers, and why did you go together?

3. Compare these two experiences. What words would you use to describe each of them?

4. What aspects of Paul's relationship with the Philippian church emerge in Philippians Chapter 1? Identify key words or phrases that indicate the nature of their partnership and community.

5. When have you experienced Christian community most deeply? Who are the persons who come to mind? Give thanks to God for each of them.

6. What can you do to make these experiences of community more frequent so that they become a way of life for you and those around you?

7. How does your prayer life incorporate other members of your community?

Prayer

Loving creator,
your design for us is life together.
In the arms of your Son, Jesus Christ,
we are embraced in a community
shaped by the cross.
Draw us nearer to you and to each other,
through the power of your Holy Spirit.
Amen.

Focus for the Week

Take a few moments each day to slow down and pray for those around you. In the morning, remember and pray for those friends who are with you on your spiritual journey. During the week, write a note to two or three of them and tell them how you have been praying for them. In the evening, reflect on those companions who have blessed your life in the last twenty-four hours. Say a prayer of thanks to God for them.

Prayer and Service

Scripture: Read Philippians 2:1-11

"Adopt the attitude that was in Christ Jesus . . . "

(Philippians 2:5)

When I first started traveling to Haiti years ago, I came upon one of the best books I have read in my life: *Mountains Beyond Mountains*, by the Pulitzer Prize-winning author Tracy Kidder. It is a biography of a man named Paul Farmer, who grew up in the rural poverty of central Florida, attended Duke University as an undergraduate and then Harvard University Medical School. Farmer now divides his time between Harvard, where he teaches, and central Haiti, where he operates a medical hospital.

I enjoy reading, but it is unusual for me to read a book more than once. I have read *Mountains Beyond Mountains* three times. It is passionate and funny, and it is an extraordinary portrait of the Haitian people. One passage in the book continues to speak to me. In it, Farmer reflects on the dilemma of living a somewhat divided life: teaching at a place like Harvard, where most everyone is successful, and practicing in Haiti, where most everyone is desperate. The passage occurs toward the end of the book, recounting the time when an emaciated young man is flown to Boston for treatment with funds raised by Farmer's nonprofit organization. Later the young man would die, and one of the staff would question whether this was an appropriate expenditure of the twenty thousand dollars it took to fly him from Haiti. This gets back to Paul Farmer, and he has a conversation about it with the author, Tracy Kidder:

> "It was a shame you had to spend so much, given what else you could do with twenty grand."
> "Yeah, but there are so many ways of saying that," [Farmer] replies. "For example, why didn't the airline company that makes money . . . why didn't they pay for his flight? That's a way of saying it. Or how about this way? How about if I say, I have fought for *my whole life* a long defeat. How about that? How about if I said, That's all it adds up to is defeat?"
> "A long defeat."
> "I have fought the long defeat and brought other people on to fight the long defeat, and I'm not going to stop because we keep losing. Now I actually think sometimes we may *win*. I don't dislike victory . . .
> "You know, people from our background . . . we're used to being on the victory team, and actually what we're really trying to do in [Partners in Health] is to make common cause with the *losers*. Those are two very different things. We *want* to be on the winning team, but at the *risk* of turning our backs on the losers, no, it's not worth it. So you fight the long defeat."[1]

Where did Paul Farmer get the phrase, "the long defeat"? It is from his favorite book, *The Fellowship of the Ring* (Book 1 in the Lord of the Rings trilogy), where Galadriel says, "Through the ages of the world we have fought the long defeat." And the elf Galadriel had sprung from the profound imagination of J. R. R. Tolkien, who once wrote, in a letter to a friend, "I am a Christian . . . so I do not expect history to be anything but a long defeat—though it contains . . . some samples or glimpses of final victory."

The Long Defeat

The season of Lent flows into Palm/Passion Sunday, and in this time more than any other we remember that the Christian faith is about fighting the long defeat. Jesus is tested in the wilderness (Matthew 4:1-11; Mark 1:12-13; Luke 4:1-13), and then the events of Jesus' triumphant entry into Jerusalem become a story about Jesus' arrest and death on a cross. Jesus is betrayed by one of his disciples, denied by another, and abandoned by the rest. This journey toward the cross began when Jesus set his face to Jerusalem (Luke 9:51), but in truth it began even earlier. We can see the steps on this path when those worshiping in Nazareth drive Jesus from their town (Luke 4:14-30), and we can see them when Herod slaughters the innocents shortly after Jesus is born (Matthew 2:16-18). Lent and Holy Week are the culmination of the events of Jesus' life, which is in many ways a long defeat. Lent and Holy Week are the natural and inevitable destination, maybe, of the one who gained so much of his identity by reading the suffering servant passages in Isaiah: "It was certainly our sickness that he carried, and our sufferings that he bore"(Isaiah 53:4). It is the way of Jesus, this road of suffering:

> "But he emptied himself
>   by taking the form of a slave
>   and by becoming like human beings.
> When he found himself in the form of a human,
>   he humbled himself by becoming obedient to the point
>   of death,
>   even death on a cross." (Philippians 2:7-8)

"Adopt the attitude that was in Christ Jesus," the apostle Paul writes to the Philippians (2:5). And so those who follow Jesus will, like him, encounter grief, sorrow, and suffering. We can choose to become passive, stoic, or cynical all of this, saying with bitterness that "only the good die young," as the popular song expressed it. Or, in the words of Tolkien and Paul Farmer, we can learn to fight the long defeat, doing so with the attitude of Jesus.

Why do we fight the long defeat?

On Christmas Eve for over twenty years I would stand in the center of the sanctuary, the room filled with candlelight and the faces of people standing side by side, and I would repeat the words of Howard Thurman about the work of Christmas:

> "To find the lost,
> To heal the broken,
> To feed the hungry,
> To release the prisoner,
> To rebuild the nations,
> To bring peace among brothers."[2]

These are inspiring words, and I think Thurman gets it exactly right. And yet, some of the lost stay lost, some of the broken remain broken, and some children still go to bed hungry. Some prisoners are released and then return to prison. Some nations are rebuilt only to be crushed again. Violence and warfare continue among those who should live as brothers and sisters.

So what do you do? Do you chalk up the words of that poem to the idealism of a great preacher and prophet, admitting that in the real world we must settle for less? Do you give up, reasoning that the benefit of such Christmas work is not worth the cost?

Do you throw in the towel and have a seat on the sidelines? Or, do you fight the long defeat?

We fight the long defeat for a simple reason: We are followers of Jesus, and Jesus constantly made common cause with those the world called losers. Jesus reached out to gentiles, lepers, the poor, children, women, the sick, the mentally ill, and the hungry. Why did he do that? It was his mission in life; the Son of Man came to seek and save that which is lost.

None of this sat well with the religious authorities, and it was finally what got Jesus killed. You can feel the tension building in the Gospels. Brace yourself! It all begins to unravel in the readings for Holy Week, the last chapters of any Gospel, take your pick. In many congregations this is the drama performed on Good Friday evening in the Tenebrae service. We hear the last words of Jesus, spoken from the cross. We sense the deepening darkness, and we feel the impending finality of the long defeat.

Why such extravagance? Why such a gift, poured out in that way, God dying for the ungodly? Why did Jesus offer such a great sacrifice for a world that had turned its back on him? Surely there was a better use of the Incarnation than death on a cross, just as there were better ways to use twenty thousand dollars than flying a young man to Boston to die. And yet, Jesus fights the long defeat. Jesus makes common cause with the losers. Why does he do this? Listen to the explanation of Will Willimon:

> The significant thing is that Jesus willingly accepted the destiny toward which his actions drove him, willingly endured the world's response to its salvation. . . . And he did it for Love: the cross is not what God demands of Jesus for our sin but rather what Jesus got for bringing the love of God so close to sinners like us.[3]

Sinners like us . . . finally the motive for such an extravagant, costly grace is the life of each person, including you and me and that young Haitian lying on an operating table. Each person matters to God: a young woman struggling to find herself in this world; a man at midlife wondering if he has made the right sacrifices or if they have simply been compromises; a woman at the end of life who also feels betrayed or abandoned. On the cross Jesus makes common cause with them, with us. On the cross Jesus refuses to turn his back on them, or on us. It is, in the words of Wesley's hymn, "love's redeeming work":

"To find the lost,
To heal the broken,
To feed the hungry,
To release the prisoner,
To rebuild the nations,
To bring peace among brothers."

That redeeming work of love is not only our making the world a better place, not only what we can do in this world. More crucially—there is that word, related to the cross—more crucially it is what God does in us and for us. We are lost and broken; we are hungry and imprisoned; we inhabit the ruined cities and live with our own irreconcilable differences. The cross is what Jesus got for bringing the love of God so close to sinners like us.

Becoming Servants

How do we fight the long defeat? We must learn to become servants. People like us, we are used to being on the victory team. But in Lent, as we move toward a garden, a cross, and an empty tomb, we journey once again into the heart of darkness, into the mystery of our faith, into the clearest image we have of the long defeat:

"he emptied himself
by taking the form of a slave
and by becoming like human beings"

The Son of God became like us, someone in the early church observed, so that we might become like him. He became a servant so that we might become servants. He took up the cross so that we might take what one of my divinity school professors, Robert Cushman, called "the cruciform life." In becoming Christians we enter the lifelong process of becoming like Jesus, and that changes us. We become servants. We begin to see the world differently.

Prayer is a chief way in which we learn to see the world as God sees it. It is no coincidence that Jesus prays frequently throughout the Gospels, or that Paul's prayers permeate his letters. Through prayer, we come to know and imitate the mind of Christ. And we learn to become servants ourselves.

I once lived in a city where two hospitals were approaching a merger. One of the themes in the local newspaper was the impact of the merger on the workforce. The question was posed, "What will this mean for the staffs?" A housekeeping staff member at one hospital was interviewed. She responded, "I'm not worried; there is always going to be a mess to clean up. Somebody's going to have to do it."

I hear echoes, in her wisdom, of the long defeat. But even more deeply, I hear the voice of a servant, of one who is in the process of becoming like Jesus. What does it mean to become like Jesus? We get a clear vision in the Philippians passage for today. In Philippians 2:1-11, we see God's nature, which is to give, and the mind of Christ, which is to serve. It is clearly visible. How could we miss it?

A cruciform life is a servant's life. A Christian life, one shaped by the cross, is a self-emptying life. Jesus identified with us. He emptied himself. He became like us so that we might become like him.

As the bishop of Florida, I have come to know and appreciate the Methodist bishop of Cuba, Ricardo Pereira. The church in Cuba has undergone great persecution and also a profound renewal. I asked Bishop Pereira once if he could describe what had happened in this amazing transformation. He told the story of two men who had prayed all night for the gift of the Holy Spirit. At the conclusion of that intense time of prayer, they began to speak in tongues. They then came to the bishop and asked him, "Now that we have received the gift of the Holy Spirit, what position can you give us?" Bishop Pereira reflected for a moment, and then he pointed them toward a mop leaning against the wall. He then said, "Now that you have had this powerful spiritual experience, you can mop the floor of the sanctuary!" The implication is clear: A deeper experience of God fits us for a life of more humble service.

Shaped by the Cross

It helps to take a broader view of what is happening here in the Scripture. From the hand of a Christian pastor (Paul), writing years later to one of his first congregations, a congregation that he helped to found, we have the letter to the church at Philippi. This letter is filled with practical advice. Paul knows the congregation, and himself, well. He warns them against the deadly sins that inflict any community: self-centeredness, conceit, grumbling. One thinks she is the center of the universe, while another is puffed up with pride and still another is what we might call a "whiner"!

Paul pleads with his readers, and with us, to strive toward the fruit of the Christian life. And at the conclusion of Philippians 1, he encourages the Philippians to "live together in a manner worthy of Christ's gospel" (1:27). In addition, he appeals to them to "stand firm, united in one spirit and mind as you struggle together to remain faithful to the gospel" (1:27).

Into this appeal for unity Paul introduces a hymn about Christ with the words "Adopt the attitude that was in Christ Jesus" (2:5). The hymn is set in the context of our need for unity. In the previous chapter, we saw the deep need for partnership: "If you want to travel far, walk together." Unity was critical for the early Christian movement, just as it is crucial in our own life together. But the Philippian church was conflicted; though some were genuine, others were speaking and serving out of envy or rivalry. And so Paul urges them to be of the same mind, to live in one accord.

It is often true that our response to conflict is one of either avoidance or denial. And yet I am convinced that the Christian faith gives us the resources to move more deeply into our conflict, so that it might be transformed and transcended. We live together in Christian communities even amidst division, because of realities such as love and encouragement, both of which Paul mentions in Philippians 2:1.

"Complete my joy," Paul writes, "by thinking the same way, having the same love, being united, and agreeing with each other" (2:2). Such unity is possible when an even greater reality is present: servanthood. We are united when we strive to serve one another. Servanthood is grounded in humility, in our being there for and with others. But even more deeply and profoundly, it is incarnate in the "downward mobility" of God. This God, through Jesus Christ, "empties himself" and takes the form of a servant (2:7). God became a servant, and as followers of Christ we must likewise serve one another. It is in this humble service that unity is possible.

In Lent we become aware that our lives, if they are taking the form of Christ, are being shaped by the cross. The cross casts its shadow over the forty days of Lent. We sing about the cross that Jesus carries and we wonder if Jesus must carry the cross alone. We yearn for a church that is more Christ-centered, which is to say, more cross-centered. We confess that many of our struggles, difficulties, and tensions are the result of the distance at which we live from the cross.

To read the first few verses of the second chapter of Philippians is to confront the one who is our judge and our hope. He judges us simply in the life that he lives—a cruciform life. He judges us in his willingness to empty himself, to embrace the long defeat. He judges us in his obedience unto death, even death on a cross (2:8).

And yet, we acknowledge that Jesus is also our hope.

> "Therefore, God highly honored him
>   and gave him a name above all names,
> so that at the name of Jesus everyone
>   in heaven, on earth, and under the earth might bow
> and every tongue confess that
>   Jesus Christ is Lord, to the glory of God the Father."
>
> (Philippians 2:9-11)

Our hope is in the one who transforms conflict into peace, despair into hope, death into life, a cross into an empty tomb, and the long defeat into victory. In Lent, our knees bow and our tongues confess the lordship of our servant Jesus.

Questions for Reflection and Discussion

1. How is the Christian life a "long defeat" in your own experience? In today's world?
2. How is the mission of Jesus Christ also the mission of the church?
3. What do you feel as you shift your focus from Jesus dying for sinners to Jesus bringing God's love close to "sinners like us"?
4. As you read Philippians 2:1-11, what relationship do you see between service and unity?
5. When has someone else served you in a way that reminded you of Jesus?
6. How does your prayer life reflect the attitude of a servant?
7. What role does prayer play in service?

Prayer

Make us one, O God,
through the example of our descending and ascending Lord Jesus Christ:
fill our minds with his passion for service to this world
and shape our communities into his likeness.
Amen.

Focus for the Week

We often find ourselves in families, communities, or
congregations that are in the midst of conflict or division.
Each day this week, pray about one such conflict or division.
In your prayers, try to see others as God sees them and
yourself as God sees you. As you conclude your prayer, read
Philippians 2:5-11. How is God calling you to become a
servant in your circumstances?

1. From *Mountains Beyond Mountains*, by Tracy Kidder (Random House, 2003); page 288.

2. From "The Work of Christmas," by Howard Thurman in *The Mood of Christmas and Other Celebrations* (Friends United Press, 1985); page 23.

3. From *Why Jesus?* By William H. Willimon (Abingdon Press, 2010); page 110.

Prayer and Formation

Scripture: Read Philippians 2:12-30

"Carry out your own salvation with fear and trembling. God is the one who enables you both to want and to actually live out his good purposes" (Philippians 2:12-13).

After exhorting the Philippians to have the same mind that was in Christ Jesus (Philippians 2:5-11), Paul writes, "Carry out your own salvation with fear and trembling" (2:12).

When we read a command such as this—to carry out or work out our own salvation—we are challenged on a number of levels. The presence of the words *work* or *carry out* leads us to hear this in light of our own human agency: something we must achieve or accomplish. We imagine that we are supplying the effort, the energy, the initiative. It is about us, and there is a cause and effect relationship between the goal and the outcome.

This is a common posture at the heart of the good life, even the moral life, but the problem lies in the focus of the work in Paul's image. How are we to work out our own salvation? Or to put it differently, what is the relationship between "works" and "salvation"? In the history of Christian thought, this question has been an important one. Theologians have struggled through the centuries to understand how our works contribute to our salvation, or not!

The apostle Paul was a fierce advocate for the separation of work and salvation. We are saved by God's grace, not by anything we do, he says in Ephesians 2:8. But the reflection upon this verse and its implications goes far beyond the matter of significant terms in church history, or even the doctrinal controversies that have separated our denominations and traditions. It has a direct bearing on the shape of our faith as individuals and as a faith community.

Either/Or

It is often the case that we gravitate toward what some call "either/or" or "all or nothing" thinking. We are either in control of an activity, or we withdraw and do not participate at all. We are totally responsible, or we accept no responsibility whatsoever. We are intensely interested, or we quickly become bored. This is the case in many aspects of our lives, is it not? And it can carry over into the spiritual life. We believe that God is in control of all things, and so we become passive. We stop growing in our faith because, we reason, it won't make a difference in our salvation. Or we believe the alternative, that it's more about our actions than God's. We think, as the cliché goes, that "if it is to be, it's up to me," and we push God toward the margins.

We may come to believe that it is either about prayer or action, prayer being the reliance upon God over all things, action being our responsibility for the outcome. This leads to a bifurcated vision of life, in which prayer and action become mutually exclusive. We label others as either mystics or activists;

we judge them to be sectarian or compromised. We ourselves pray without acting, or we act without praying. When we read Paul's words in Philippians 2:12, we tend to read them in light of this segmented vision of the world. If it must be prayer or action, Paul's words seem to fall in the action camp. And so we are tempted to believe that it all depends on us. We are to carry out or to work out our own salvation.

Such an understanding leads us down the path of self-help and self-destruction. I have known good and moral people who could not easily distinguish their participation in a civic club on Friday from their involvement in a congregation on Sunday. Along the way they had been taught to be good and moral people, and the pursuit of this ideal had become fused with their vision of what it meant to be a disciple of Jesus Christ. As a pastor for thirty years, I have also known the temptation to blur the boundaries of citizenship and discipleship, good works and faith. It can become, in the language of the Celtic contemplative Esther de Waal, the temptation to be relevant, to be spectacular, and to be powerful.

How do we resist this temptation, which was Jesus' own temptation in the Gospels (Matthew 4:1-11; Luke 4:1-13)?

We may begin with the knowledge that God saves us apart from our works, as Paul so adamantly maintained and Christian tradition has affirmed. But over the course of following Jesus over a long span of time, we may in time come to believe that God is leaving much of this work up to us. It often feels like God is at some distance from us, saying, "Work this out on your own!" And so, perhaps, we make the attempt. We work hard. We do our best. We give our most earnest effort.

At times, we succeed. Others benefit and we see some results from our efforts. But it is also true that we fail, or we fall short, and we come to have anxieties and doubts. We question our own motives or look back on how little we have progressed. If salvation is our work, we wonder about the value of it all. Have we worked enough to save ourselves and others? Is salvation merely what we are able to achieve and nothing more?

This was the experience of many who came into ministry in the latter part of the twentieth century in the United States. Inspired by the expansion of civil rights, even if much of the work remained unfinished, men and women heard the call to serve God by attempting to change the world. And many came to the conclusion, in time, that the world was powerfully resistant to change! The result was burnout and disillusionment.

When I am most grounded in my own spiritual life, I have a clear sense that life, salvation, and ministry are gifts from God. I am not the source, but I draw strength from the living waters and daily bread of God's providence. There are also times, however, when I find myself at a distance from this core truth about God and myself. I believe that my own efforts and works are essential and indeed are the determining factor in achieving a good life, in finding salvation, in serving as an effective minister, and in contributing to social change. My ministry becomes a performance, and I attempt to please either God or other people through my good works.

How does this "either/or" thinking show up in your own life? When have you been tempted to place the main responsibility of your salvation or social change on your own shoulders? When has the imperative to "carry out your own salvation" caused you to push God aside? Alternatively, how have you been tempted to avoid action, using God's control as an excuse for passivity?

Synergy

To avoid "either/or", "all or nothing" thinking is to live into the concept of synergy. *Synergy* is the reality that the whole is greater than the sum of its parts. In the Christian life, this is a helpful way of reflecting on the relationship between works and salvation. Paul hints at this: He tells the Philippians to carry out their own salvation (2:12), but in the next verse he says, "God is the one who enables you both to want and to actually live out his good purposes" (2:13). In other words, work out your own salvation, for God is at work in you! It is not human initiative, and it is not purely divine effort. In his well-known sermon on this passage, John Wesley quotes two verses of Scripture: "Without me, you can't do anything" (John 15:5), and "I can endure all these things through the power of the one who gives me strength" (Philippians 4:13). There is a synergy in which we acknowledge that God is the source of our strength, and yet God chooses to work within and through us. To borrow the words of a hymn, the Lord stoops to our weakness.[1]

In this view, prayer becomes neither the sole means of participation in the life of faith nor a tangential practice that is secondary to the real work of good in the world. Prayer acknowledges that God is at work within us, and when we pray we ask for that work to continue in our hearts and lives. And prayer acknowledges that God works through us. When we pray, we seek to align ourselves with the will of God so that we might be God's partners in the restoration of the world around us. Prayer recognizes the paradox at the heart of our faith: that we work out our own salvation, while at the same time sensing that God is at work in us.

I confess that I often want to resist this paradox. Over three decades of ministry, I have found myself caught in a web of a "works righteousness" performance: I have dwelled on the fullness of my calendar, the quality of my planning, and the achievements of my churches. Note the recurrence of the word *my*!

Such behavior has energy and momentum at its inception, but I have also discovered that it cannot be sustained. I become weary of continued exertion, disappointed in the efforts of others, and judgmental about the fruitfulness of a congregation. Love and joy, peace and patience, which are fruits of the Holy Spirit (Galatians 5:22-23), wear thin. I find that I am repeating the cycle of church history: I have forgotten that the grace of God saves me, and imagined that my works are a worthy substitute! I have missed the fullness of the gospel, the good news that God is at work in me.

Over those same decades of ministry, I can look back on my better days (which is to say when I am more attentive), and I can see that God has been at work in me. This is the grace of God. God moved in spite of my limitations. God breathed life in the midst of my exhaustion. God showed up in the successes and failures of congregational life. The treasure of the gospel is contained in earthen vessels (bodies, minds, communities) to show, Paul writes elsewhere, that the transcendent power belongs to God and not to us (2 Corinthians 4:7).

Lent is a holy season, set aside by the church, to remind us of the necessary and essential practice of self-denial. Through prayer we can empty ourselves, pouring out our desires, opinions, and vanities. As we clear out such things, we become empty vessels, with space for the grace and power of Jesus Christ to enter. In the history of Christian spirituality, this has been described as the "apophatic" way or *via negativa*. We empty ourselves so that God can fill us. As we do so, we pattern our lives and our minds after the example of Christ, who emptied himself. In human practice this is also the way of humility before God. The Book of Proverbs begins with a confession: "Wisdom begins with the fear of the LORD" (Proverbs 1:7). To fear the Lord is to allow

God to melt us, mold us, fill us, and use us, as the hymn "Spirit of the Living God" says (*The United Methodist Hymnal*, 393).

This brings us back to the rest of Philippians 2:12. We are not simply to carry out our own salvation. In Paul's language, we are to carry out our own salvation "with *fear* and *trembling*." Fear is not the avoidance of a stereotyped God who is at some distance from us and yet is angry with us; fear is humility before the one who is the source of our power. The opposite of fear is pride. Trembling is our willingness to see the image of God—the sacred—in another person. We do harm to others when we do not see them as our brothers and sisters who are also the sons and daughters of God. To tremble before them is to think more highly of them than we do of ourselves (see Philippians 2:3). A posture of fear and trembling echoes the wisdom of James: "*God stands against the proud, but favors the humble*" (4:6). Imagine what would happen in our churches if every individual and community took this to heart and put it into practice. Our churches and denominations would be characterized by mutual care, encouragement, and even admiration. Think how this would strengthen our witness to one another and to the world!

God Is at Work in Us

In the Jesuit tradition of prayer, I came across the following spiritual insight:

"A thick and shapeless tree trunk would never believe that it could become a statue, admired as a miracle of sculpture, and would never submit itself to the chisel of the sculptor, who sees by her genius what she can make of it."

This aptly captures our difficulty in letting God work within us, sometimes painfully so. Carrying out our salvation with fear and trembling means submitting ourselves to "the one who enables you both to want and to actually live out his good purposes" (Philippians 2:13). And so the question arises: How can we entrust our lives into the hands of our loving Creator, Redeemer and Sanctifier, who might well start in on our hearts with a chisel?

The answer is, in part, through prayer. When we pray, we acknowledge that we are not in complete control of our lives. We ask God to transform us, to work within us, to save us despite ourselves. We partner our efforts with the one who is at work within us, and we grow. Sometimes growth is slow, and sometimes it is painful. But remember in the process that you are being turned into a beautiful sculpture.

My wife has served as a pastor, missionary, and campus minister. In addition to these gifts, she has strong creative talents, and earlier in life she studied interior design. One summer, we were in the mountains enjoying a time of rest and renewal. As I was driving away from our cabin one afternoon, I saw a piece of furniture that had been left beside the road in our neighborhood. Clearly, the owner's intent was that someone would see it and pick it up. And so I asked myself: "Would my wife like this piece of furniture?"

I quickly turned the car in the opposite direction and returned to our cabin. I walked through the front door and asked Pam, "Would you like to see this piece of furniture?" Within seconds we were both in the car, on the way to view it more closely. We stopped and she quickly said, "We want that." And so we lifted it into our back seat, took it home, and carried it inside.

For the next few days she worked with this abandoned piece of furniture, cleaning, repairing, staining, and varnishing it. She told me that the piece of furniture had a name: It was a vanity. As she continued to repair and restore the vanity, it became something beautiful. In the end, it became a focal point in one the rooms of our small cabin.

That experience in a small way is a sign for me of the creative activity of our gracious God. Our lives are always in the process of being salvaged and restored. I am convinced that we can resist God's good intentions for us. To submit to the providence and purposes of God is an act of trust, and to trust implies a relinquishment of control.

Many of us might confess that our works, our activities, and our busyness have been a form of control. We have created elaborate plans for our own lives, relationships, communities, and institutions. And my intuition is that the results are at times stark and dramatic. Could it be that our best plans and efforts have found themselves set beside the road, without a purpose, to be discarded? And it might it be true that God is seeking to salvage our imperfections for the higher purpose of revealing what we were truly created to be and do?

The synergy of God's grace is found in the material substance of our works, our lives, and our gifts when they are placed in the hands of the One who knows and saves us. And the whole—the end result—is indeed greater than the sum of the parts. Our good works, apart from God's grace and creativity, can be motivated by self-interest. Our good works, apart from God's grace and creativity, are limited by our energy and capacity. And yet when our good works flow from the creativity and grace of God, they are transformed. God enables us to live out God's purposes for our lives, transforming even our desires so that we want to do this with the best of intentions (Philippians 2:13).

This synergy between God's grace and our works also extends to our relationships with one another. We see this when Paul speaks of being "poured out" in service to his sisters and brothers, expressing his gladness with them and inviting them to be glad with him (Philippians 2:17). We see it also when Paul speaks of Timothy and Epaphroditus later in the chapter (2:19-30). It's clear that he feels a deep love and gratitude for them and that they play an important role in his faith and ministry. We were created to live in community, and to express our faith through relationships with one another. This is at the heart of Paul's meditation in 1 Corinthians 13:1-3:

> If I speak in tongues of human beings and of angels but I don't have love, I'm a clanging gong or a clashing cymbal. If I have the gift of prophecy and I know all the mysteries and everything else, and if I have such complete faith that I can move mountains but I don't have love, I'm nothing. If I give away everything that I have and hand over my own body to feel good about what I've done but I don't have love, I receive no benefit whatsoever.

Without love, our works are in vain. Each of us receives spiritual gifts (1 Corinthians 12, 14) to be exercised within the body of Christ. And in this manner the whole is greater than the sum of the parts. Our salvation is initiated through faith in Jesus Christ, and it is sustained through membership in his body, the church. Salvation is a gift of God's grace, and it is carried out through participation in the means of grace: baptism, fasting, prayer, reading Scripture, receiving Holy Communion, support and accountability with other disciples. We don't participate in any of these means of grace alone, but together with our brothers and sisters in the church.

I sometimes forget that Paul was not writing a letter to an individual. In this instance, he was writing to the Philippian church, to a community of friends and followers of Jesus. Many of the life experiences at the heart of the letter were communal: conflict between persons, rivalry among leaders, the community's generosity in taking up a collection for Paul's material needs. They were working out their salvation as they engaged in each of these actions. And they were being called to remember that it was God who was at work in them—not just in individual hearts and lives, but in the community as a whole.

We are tempted to do this work in our own strength, apart from God. We are tempted to engage in these actions alone, apart from others. We attempt to find salvation apart from the church, and we seek to sustain our spiritual lives apart from the means of grace. Our isolation and our individualism have led us to fragmented and divided lives, and have distanced us from the sources of integrity and healing.

The creator sees that the whole is greater than the sum of the parts. A follower of Jesus, no matter how great her gifts or talents might be, is not designed to live and serve in her own strength. And another follower of Jesus, no matter how extraordinary his abilities or experiences, cannot fully mature as a disciple apart from the presence of other Christians in the body.

We were designed for communion with God, and we were created for community with one another. The story is one of transformation. God searches for us and finds us. God works with us, in a continuous process of cleansing and restoration. Over time we are shaped, repurposed for a life within God's will. And we discover, indeed, that "the one who started a good work in you will stay with you to complete the job by the day of Christ Jesus" (Philippians 1:6).

Questions for Reflection and Discussion

1. In what ways are you prone to either/or, or all-or-nothing thinking?

2. How do you understand the relationship between your own efforts and salvation by God's grace? How do Paul's words in Philippians 2 clarify or challenge your perspective?

3. How might you reword Paul's phrase "with fear and trembling" (Philippians 2:12) if you were communicating this concept to a friend?
4. How is activity and busyness a form of control in your relationship with God?
5. In your own spiritual life, what might it mean to "submit (yourself) to the chisel of the Sculptor?"
6. How is the concept of synergy relevant to your spiritual life? To the life of your community or congregation?
7. How does synergy between God's grace and your works show up in your prayer life?

Prayer

O God,
you see our need for community
and our resistance to the life we might share with one another;
you see our need for salvation
and our pride that keeps you at a distance.
Forgive us. Heal us. Restore us.
Use us in your great purpose through Jesus Christ our Savior and Lord. Amen.

Focus for the Week

God is shaping you and forming you. Seek to be more aware of the ways God is at work in you this week. Each day as you pray, take a few minutes to reflect on the challenges and progress in your spiritual life.

1. From "Spirit of God, Descend Upon My Heart," words by George Croly, *The United Methodist Hymnal* (Copyright ©1989 by The United Methodist Publishing House); 500.

Prayer and Sacrifice

Scripture: Read Philippians 3:1-11

"I have lost everything for him . . . so that I might gain Christ and be found in him" (Philippians 3:8-9).

I can remember the gathering as if it were last night. I was seated on the floor in a large room that was filled with other teenagers. A close friend had asked me to attend with him. There was singing, movement, smiling, and hugging. Most of the people there seemed to know one another. I sensed in myself a mixture of curiosity and apprehension. What would happen? The answer was not clear to me.

After a time, the leader stood in front of everyone and introduced a young man who was a big, strapping, talented football player. In comparison, I was a tall and skinny basketball player with average talent. In hindsight, I listened with a fair amount of envy. He began to speak, and the following would be a summary of his narrative:

"I used to have a lot of fun. I dated a different girl every night. I stayed out late. I ran with the fast crowd." As he spoke, his posture was animated, his voice filled with excitement. "I drank a lot and I dabbled in drugs. I was a part of the 'in' group. And then . . . and then . . ." Here his voice trailed off a bit. "And then I became a Christian. . . ." Now there was almost a note of regret in his voice and, as a therapist might write in a notebook, a flatness in his affect. "And then I became a Christian, and now I don't do any of that anymore."

The young man, having concluded his testimony, walked away from the microphone and sat down, and everyone applauded. Now at that time, I was what one might define as a "God-fearer," the term used to describe first-century Gentiles who sympathized with the Jewish religion but were not full converts. I was not quite in the household of faith, but hanging around the edges. In John Wesley's language, I was spending time on the porch, but I had no clear intention to knock on the door. Even so, intuitively I knew that this young man was talking about sacrifice. He was attempting to narrate his own life from the perspective of a sacrifice that made sense to him and to those of us who were listening.

Four decades later, I recall that evening. I have forgotten (mercifully) a great deal about my adolescent years, but I remember that evening and the story of an athlete who was reliving, in some kind of fragmented and incoherent way, the experience of the apostle Paul.

Paul's Sacrifice

In writing to the Philippians, expressing gratitude for a gift and helping the community to navigate a conflict, Paul arrived at a place in the letter where he sensed a need to become autobiographical, relating a portion of his own life story. He did so by using the image of sacrifice, recounting everything he had given up in order to follow Christ. Sacrifice was certainly a part of Paul's Scripture, the Hebrew Bible or the Old Testament.

Abraham was called to offer the sacrifice of his son Isaac (Genesis 22:1-19), and God's people would develop a tradition of bringing sacrifices to the Temple. These sacrificial practices could and would later be abused, and the prophets spoke clearly against sacrifices that were not pleasing to God. David, in one of the memorable Psalms, offers an honest confession:

> "You don't want sacrifices.
>   If I gave an entirely burned offering,
>   you wouldn't be pleased.
> A broken spirit is my sacrifice, God.
>   You won't despise a heart, God, that is broken and crushed."
>
> (Psalm 51:16-17)

Despite this passage and others like it, sacrifice remains at the heart of our faith. We no longer spill the blood of animals in ritual ceremonies, but we do give deeply of ourselves in order to follow Christ more closely. In the season of Lent we are especially called to self-denial, to the common and almost familiar practice of "giving up something." The options for doing so can range from the meaningful to the trivial. Some Christians fast, or eat moderately, or seek to consume in solidarity with those who live a more sustainable lifestyle. This is a form of sacrifice, and it is derived from the deeper traditions of the Old and New Testaments. In the Old Testament, God's people wandered in the wilderness for forty years, and they were sustained by the sufficiency of daily manna (Exodus 16). In the New Testament, Jesus was driven into the wilderness for forty days, and there he fasted and prayed (Matthew 4:1-11; Luke 4:1-13). These patterns and practices shaped the Christian observance of Lent in the early church, as persons prepared themselves for baptism and entrance into the community (again recalling the journey to the Promised Land). They reflected on their sin and the need for repentance and cleansing, which is embodied in the Gospels in the life of John the Baptist, who also spent time in the wilderness.

This deep tradition of sacrificial practice shaped the life of the apostle Paul, as well as how he understood the trajectory of his own life. And so he narrates the experience that led to a place of authority and leadership in the lives of the Philippians:

> "I was circumcised on the eighth day.
> I am from the people of Israel and the tribe of Benjamin.
> I am a Hebrew of the Hebrews.
> With respect to observing the Law, I'm a Pharisee.
> With respect to devotion to the faith, I harassed the church.
> With respect to righteousness under the Law, I'm blameless."
> (Philippians 3:5-6)

It is helpful to reconstruct what Paul's words would have meant to the Philippians. That he was "circumcised on the eighth day" signified that he was not an adult convert to Judaism. The law held that Jewish males would be circumcised as infants on the eighth day after their birth (see Genesis 17:10-14 and Leviticus 12:3). Paul is telling the Philippians that he has been a Jew his whole life. I have often listened to active participants in congregations tell me that they have been members of those churches since birth! Paul understands the weight of his upbringing: His parents were a devout couple who saw to his ritual faith observance from the beginning.

In addition, Paul was an Israelite both religiously and ethnically, and he was from the "tribe of Benjamin." Being able to trace his lineage to a tribe of Israel demonstrates Paul's pedigree, but there is also significance in the specific tribe of Benjamin. Benjamin was the youngest of Jacob's sons, the last one born to Jacob's favored wife Rachel. In addition, Benjamin was the only son born in Canaan, the Promised Land (Genesis 35:16-20). Later, Saul, the first king of Israel, would trace his lineage from the tribe of Benjamin (1 Samuel 9:1-2). Paul truly was, as he claims, a "Hebrew of the Hebrews." As such, he would have retained the heritage and language of his faith. It's likely that the Hebrew language of the Old Testament would have been transmitted from generation to generation in his family home.

In Paul's description of this past, the first three sentences refer to his family of origin and religious heritage. The next three sentences speak more about his personal commitments and moral behavior. He was a Pharisee, and in his everyday life he consciously sought to keep the laws of holiness and purity. As one who persecuted the church, he not only supported those who shared his convictions but also opposed those who were engaged in a different way of living and believing. He regarded this as evidence of his zeal and devotion, his willingness to go to great lengths to keep himself and his community upright and pure in the law. He sincerely believed that one could fulfill the requirements of the Torah and that he had indeed met those requirements.

When we pause for a moment to reflect on Paul's pedigree, we discover that it is indeed impressive. It includes aspects of what would contribute to an esteemed status in our own time: privilege, class, stability, discipline, and integrity. Most of us would consider Paul's life story to be one of significance. In the economic language of assets and liabilities, we would consider these attributes of his to be assets. And yet at precisely this point, Paul's narrative takes a turn: "These things were my assets," he writes, and in the very next breath he describes his willingness to sacrifice them: "I wrote them off as a loss for the sake of Christ" (Philippians 3:7).

The sacrifice, for Paul, is considerable. Often in his letters Paul encourages his readers to imitate him (see Philippians 4:9).

When we give thought to those behaviors we might "give up for Lent," we often choose ones that are well within our reach. These "sacrifices" may be achievable and may represent areas of life that we can easily discard. Here I am the chief of sinners: In past Lenten seasons I have chosen to eliminate sweets and sodas from my diet, and I have reduced the amount of time I have spent with social media. These are healthy changes, and they may even contribute to a more sound body, mind, and spirit. But they fall far short of the sacrifice of the apostle Paul. He has given up core aspects of his identity and has radically reversed his religious commitments. And indeed, this becomes a part of his powerful testimony. What would it mean for us to imitate Paul in making such a sacrifice, laying aside important parts of ourselves in order to embrace our identity in Christ more completely?

Nothing of Importance Ever Happens Without Sacrifice

Earlier in this chapter, I shared an experience of testimony in a gathering of young people. As I began to participate in the church, I came to hear another, simpler narrative from women and men who shared their faith journeys. It proceeded along these lines:

I was living a terrible life.
I was an awful person in a number of respects.
I really had no options and no future.
Along the way I had an encounter with Jesus Christ.
After accepting him, I have been changed.
I now have the experience of a wonderful life.

I want to honor the truthfulness of authentic testimony, and indeed this is the journey for many from the old life to the new.

But Paul's life experience was very different. He was doing quite well, thank you. He had a plan, he had been prepared, and he was focused. Then he was blinded by the light of Christ (Acts 9:1-31). He would later receive his sight again and with it a new conviction and a renewed power. The gospel is for the strong as well as the weak, and a part of its relevance can be in teaching the strong that there is a power greater than their strength!

To give away power is very difficult. None of us likes to do this. To give up or give away anything of value is hard. But that is sacrifice. So what can sacrifice mean, for us? I often return to the brief wisdom of an older preacher, who shared an insight with me years ago: "Nothing of importance ever happens without sacrifice."

Spiritual growth requires sacrifice. Putting ourselves in a place to hear God's voice, to seek God's will, may involve rising early in the morning for a quiet time of prayer and study. The spiritual growth of children and young people requires that we (as adults) discipline ourselves to put them in places where their faith can thrive and mature. It is much the same way with any form of growth and learning. In our family, our children have had piano and viola lessons, gymnastics and volleyball practices, Latin classes and choir rehearsals. These experiences in the lives of our children have been important. But we as parents played a role, too. We signed sign them up, drove them to and from practice, inquired about their homework, and attended meets and recitals. These experiences required our children to be disciplined, but they also required us as parents to be disciplined as well.

Perhaps that word *discipline* is a good way to understand our word *sacrifice*. We make sacrifices to put our children in places where they will learn and grow. We do the same for ourselves. Spiritual growth requires that we sacrifice something. If we are to grow spiritually, it will happen because of disciplined intention.

Relationships also require sacrifice. Think of a marriage between two persons. They stand together before God and make promises to each other, rehearsing the church's language of sacrifice. Across a lifetime, God willing, they will live into their promises: in the welcoming and raising of children; in navigating disappointments and even betrayals; in caring for one another "in sickness and in health"; in allowing their priorities and values to merge from two into one.

I recall here an experience from pastoral ministry that reveals my own shortsightedness. I received word at the church that a member of the congregation had died. I had served there as a pastor for a number of years, and I did not recognize the name. I took the name and address and traveled to their home. Along the way, I will confess, I formed a judgment about the family. I came to the conclusion that since I had not come to know them, the church was not a high priority in their lives.

I entered the home and met the surviving husband. He shared some of their experience in the past few years. The two had enjoyed a long and happy marriage. But in the last years, his wife had made the journey through Alzheimer's and dementia. Through the week there had been caregivers, but Sunday morning was the one time he did not have someone from the outside there. And besides, he knew that by his wife's side was where he had wanted to be. "Now that she is gone," he said, "you will see more of me at church. But the past few years, I believe this was where God wanted me to be."

When I opened my car and sat down, I closed my eyes and asked God to forgive me for my quickness to judgment. And then I began to reflect, as I drove away, on the power of that husband's sacrifice.

Like relationships between individuals, community also requires sacrifice. For a few years, I enjoyed hiking about once a year at Mt. LeConte, near Gatlinburg, Tennessee, in the Great

Smoky Mountains. At the bottom of the mountain, there were always people horsing around, throwing Frisbees, drinking beer, and sharing picnics. The hike would begin, and the route went up to a little over sixty-five hundred feet. It took sacrifice to reach the top of the mountain: There were blisters, rainstorms, and moments when breathing became difficult. There were even bears! But, upon arriving at the peak of Mt. LeConte, there was an extraordinary sense of community. We had all sacrificed something in order to get there. And we had all accomplished something of significance together.

That is what sacrifice is about, accomplishing something of significance together. When I served as a pastor, I would often take a moment, in the middle of busy week or on a quiet Saturday morning, to walk into the church sanctuary. These spaces were built through the sacrifices of men and women. They were the result of prayers and dreams, offerings, and perseverance. They became realities as faithful followers of Jesus Christ acted upon a calling to accomplish something of significance together.

The church makes sacrifices to come and live together, but it is not our sacrifices alone that shape our community. The cross, the sacrifice made by Jesus, stands at the center of who we are. When we sacrifice something of ourselves to embrace our identity in Christ, we participate in the thing of eternal significance that he accomplished on the cross. Paul does not simply lay aside his assets because he no longer has use for them. Rather, he regards them as nothing "so that I might gain Christ and be found in him" (Philippians 3:8-9). He sacrifices lesser things in order to gain knowledge of Jesus Christ, which he regards as a "superior value" (3:8). By his sacrifice, Paul participates in the sufferings of Christ, "being conformed to his death so that I may perhaps reach the goal of the resurrection of the dead" (3:10-11). Paul draws near to the cross so that he may attain the resurrection that is on the other side of it. We are called to do the same, through our sacrifices entering into community with Christ and with one another in Christ.

We All Make Sacrifices

We often think of sacrifice as carving out a little time, a little money, a little attention for God. And yet, isn't it true that we all make sacrifices? Think of all the sacrifices you make for things that are less than God: a car, a house, an education, a career, entertainment. Doesn't it require sacrifice of some sort to possess these things? What if God is saying, to us: You've been sacrificing yourself on lesser altars, giving yourself to realities that are inferior to the God of Abraham, Isaac, and Jacob? What if God watches us and mourns as we invest ourselves in matters only to discover later that they are false idols?

It is not that we are not sacrificial, disciplined people. It is that we are prone to give ourselves to lesser gods. I served for a number of years in a large city that was a banking center for the world. A woman came into my office one afternoon and said, "I'm not going to give the rest of my life to corporate America." She knew that she was making sacrifices to something other than God. And her revelation called to mind the wisdom of one of the desert fathers:

"Do not give your heart to that which cannot satisfy your heart."[1]

Many of us are tempted to sacrifice ourselves for purposes that are not enduring, lasting, or eternal. Prayer can help us reshape our priorities and make sacrifices only for the one who is worthy of them. Through discipline, we can sacrifice in order to speak with God daily and hear God's voice in the silence or through the Scriptures. We can become more like Christ in our willingness to give ourselves for others, making sacrifices for our partners and for our community. Prayer helps us count the cost of discipleship and, perhaps more importantly, recognize the deep cost of refusing to follow Christ in our lives and in our world.

Paul had reached the place in his journey, after much reflection and prayer, where he had counted the cost of discipleship. He writes about the identity and status he is laying aside:

> These things were my assets, but I wrote them off as a loss for the sake of Christ. But even beyond that, I consider everything a loss in comparison with the superior value of knowing Christ Jesus my Lord. I have lost everything for him, but what I lost I think of as sewer trash, so that I might gain Christ and be found in him. . . . The righteousness that I have comes from knowing Christ, the power of his resurrection, and the participation in his sufferings.
>
> (Philippians 3:7-10)

As Paul lays aside his status, he makes a significant sacrifice in order to know Christ and the power of his Resurrection and the fellowship of his sufferings. It is a sacrifice made upon a worthy altar, indeed, the very place where God has first given himself for us. As Paul would write to the Galatians:

"I have been crucified with Christ; and it is no longer I who live, but Christ who lives in me. And the life I now live in the flesh I live by faith in the Son of God, who loved me and gave himself for me"(Galatians 2:19-20, NRSV).

Questions for Reflection and Discussion

1. Have you shared your testimony (faith story) with another person or a group? What was that experience like?
2. If you were to make a list of your privileges and achievements, where would you begin? What would be on the list?

3. How do your privileges and achievements relate to your faith? Would you consider them to be assets or liabilities?

4. In the season of Lent, do you find it meaningful to "give up" something? Why or why not? Have you given up something during Lent this year?

5. Can you recall a significant sacrifice that was made on your behalf by another person? How did it affect you?

6. What sacrifices have you made in following Christ?

7. How is God calling you to sacrifice more in order to "gain Christ and be found in him"?

Prayer

Lord Jesus Christ,
you gave your life for us
on the hard wood of the cross.
We gaze upon your sacrifice
with awe and wonder.
Help us also to lead lives
shaped in the form of a cross,
so that we might give ourselves for others. Amen.

Focus for the Week

As you pray, focus on what sacrifices you must make to grow spiritually. Ask God what you can do to "gain Christ and be found in him." Ask what sacrifices will strengthen your relationships and your Christian community. Throughout the week, take steps to put these sacrifices into practice, trusting God for courage and guidance.

1. From *The Sayings of the Desert Fathers: The Alphabetical Collection*, trans. by Benedicta Ward, SLG (Cistercian Publications, 1984); page 178.

Prayer and Perseverance

Scripture: Read Philippians 3:12-16

"I forget about the things behind me and reach out for the things ahead of me" (Philippians 3:13).

Recently I began to track down the answer to a question: How long does it take a person to form a new habit? Naturally, I went to the source of knowledge in our time, the Internet! As it turns out, I found a number of different answers: twenty-one days, sixty-six days, thirty days, and other responses in that general range. There was also the skeptical response, perhaps accounting for human factors or differing environments, that there is no set number of days!

I gave some thought to this question because in Philippians 3 the apostle Paul writes of a goal, a destination in his spiritual journey toward Christ. How long, I wondered, does it take to shape this journey with regular patterns, habits that aid one's steady progress? I then framed the question around the church's practice of Lent, in which we devote forty days to self-examination, self-denial, and spiritual growth. In Lent (a word that comes from the Anglo-Saxon term *lencten*, in reference to the lengthening days of spring), we seek to form new habits and practices in our spiritual journeys. In doing so, we follow in the steps of the apostle Paul, who writes about his own faith:

> It's not that I have already reached this goal or have already been perfected, but I pursue it, so that I may grab hold of it because Christ grabbed hold of me for just this purpose. Brothers and sisters, I myself don't think I've reached it, but I do this one thing: I forget about the things behind me and reach out for the things ahead of me. The goal I pursue is the prize of God's upward call in Christ Jesus. (Philippians 3:12-14)

In Chapter 4, we reflected on Paul's narration of his past (Philippians 3:5-6). His autobiography is both impressive and problematic. Paul's description of his past gave the Philippians a glimpse into his identity, his convictions, and his values. Yet even with such attributes, he did not know Christ. For that reason he was willing to count any of his merits as a loss for the sake of knowing Christ, the power of his resurrection, and the fellowship of his suffering (3:7-11).

This deep mystical knowing is at the heart of Paul's identity, but he quickly comments to the Philippians that he has not arrived at this spiritual goal (Philippians 3:12). In confessing that he has not yet reached the goal, Paul acknowledges his humanity. He writes elsewhere, to the church at Corinth:

> We have this treasure in clay pots so that the awesome power belongs to God and doesn't come from us. We are experiencing all kinds of trouble, but we aren't crushed. We are confused, but we aren't depressed. We are harassed, but we aren't abandoned. We are knocked down, but we aren't knocked out.
> (2 Corinthians 4:7-9)

The path toward holiness (or maturity or perfection) necessarily includes an element of transparency. In my spiritual journey, some of my mentors, the holy men and women in my own life, have been marked not only by an overflowing of love toward God and neighbor, but they have also been persons who are utterly transparent. This transparency is marked by a willingness to claim who they have been created to be, and conversely, not to pretend to be someone they are not. It has come at the cost of making peace with their finitude and limitations, and it manifests itself as a willingness to reveal wounds and scars.

On the Way to Perfection

When the apostle Paul likens the life of a follower of Jesus to a treasure contained in a clay pot, he is making an important distinction. It is what the vessel contains that matters the most, not the vessel itself. As an analogy, we can consider the chalice and patin used in the church to serve Communion. The chalice contains the blood of Christ. Yet as beautiful (or as flawed) as the chalice might be, it remains (only) a chalice. The patin is the surface upon which the body of Christ is placed. It may be an exquisite piece of pottery, or it may be made of ordinary earthen materials. We do not treasure the chalice or the patin. They are simply vessels that contain the outward and visible sign of Christ's life, his grace for us.

This is also true with us as human beings. The awesome power belongs to God, not to us. We are flawed in ways that we know and ways we do not know. Yet the indwelling Christ abides with us, in us, and among us. The distinction keeps us humble, while the promise of God's presence gives us confidence and encourages us in further growth. Through our lives we can affirm, with Paul, that we have not reached the goal, but we are striving towards it. We have not been perfected, but by the grace of God we are on the way. In my own tradition, United Methodism, we say that we are on the way to perfection.

The concept of perfection is a complex one. Alexander Maclaren, the ninteeth-century British interpreter of Scripture, observed: "The measure of our perfection will be the consciousness of our imperfection—a paradox, but a great truth. It is plain enough that it will be so. Conscience becomes more sensitive as we get nearer right" (Expositions of Holy Scripture: Philippians). The common notion of perfection as the absence of moral flaws or errors in judgment and behavior is foreign to the biblical witness. Instead, perfection is progress in maturation and a desire to attain the end for which we are created by God.

There is, in Paul's reflection on his own spiritual life, an awareness that he is on a journey. This journey flows from the past (his heritage) to the future (his destination). The journey has taken him from his assumptions about himself and his enemies, through the experience of a radical intervention, to a new way of seeing. Paul can only look back and marvel at where he has been and where he is going. He is on a purposeful journey, and he uses the image of an athlete who strives toward a goal or a prize to describe this idea for his readers (Philippians 3:13). As one translation puts it, Paul presses toward the goal "straining forward to what lies ahead" (NRSV).

I have friends and family members who run marathons. These events, once scheduled, become a central focus in their lives. They plan for the future, setting aside the date of the race and caring for all the details that surround the event. They also prepare each day and week, running increasingly longer distances as the date draws near. They understand that their bodies are changing; they endure stress, strain, and fatigue in order to develop a greater capacity to complete the marathon.

For many of them, the guiding mental image is crossing the finish line, finishing the race, and gaining a sense of accomplishment and completion. A clear focus on their goal guides them through the process of change and growth.

In a simple way, this image is helpful in thinking about our lives as followers of Jesus. We are always in motion, being called from stability and stasis (even from stuckness!) to the pursuit of a closer and deeper relationship with Jesus Christ. As another example, we can consider the implications of this text for our communities of faith. Living and vital churches are always in a state of change, adapting to their environments, evaluating their effectiveness, managing mid-course corrections. It is true that many congregations resist such change, remaining the same as their communities are transformed around them. The result can be a geographical proximity but a spiritual and missional distance, ending in decline, irrelevance, and even the death of the congregation.

In the same manner, the individual Christian can choose to remain where he or she is—content with the same practices, relationships, understandings, and convictions—yet this can often be our way of (unintentionally) resisting the movement of the Holy Spirit. Paul certainly experienced deep change in his own inner self, in his understanding of those with ethnic and religious differences, and in his life purpose. We often speak of "standing firm in our biblical convictions"; it is ironic that the primary author of much of the New Testament underwent profound intellectual, spiritual, and missional changes across his lifetime! For Paul, remaining true to his faith and calling meant opening his convictions to change through the Spirit's leading.

To "strain forward" is to experience the pain of change, and yet it is the essential process of growth, whether one is an athlete or a student. To pursue a spiritual discipline during the season of Lent is to move through these forty days, knowing that we will become more like Jesus Christ as we walk with him into experiences of solitude, emptiness, and reliance on God. To adopt a practice of prayer is to grow into it and within it, allowing the practice to shape us even as we move through changing circumstances in life. In the Old Testament, Israel was also called to become a movement, from an enslaved people to those who would taste freedom. But a necessary facet of that journey was a time spent in the wilderness. Jesus would repeat this pattern—he would spend time in the wilderness and later would set his face toward Jerusalem (Luke 9:51)—and he calls us to follow him. In the process, Israel and Jesus (the new Israel) would become new people. And so it is with the church. As a community of disciples, we are always on the move, always being changed. This is disruptive, yet it is the way that leads to life.

Forgetting About the Things Behind

It may seem paradoxical that the apostle Paul gives great care and attention to rehearsing his past and reminding the Philippians of his identity, only to insist that, in his journey of being a disciple, he is forgetting the things behind him (Philippians 3:13)! Despite this paradox, many of us live in this same tension. I am the beneficiary of the blessings, provisions, and gifts of family, friends, and mentors along the way. I am surely the product of a number of advantages, privileges, and opportunities that have also come to me. But the awareness of this past may or may not contribute to my progress as a disciple of Jesus.

In Paul's confession, one can sense the weight of this history in both positive and negative terms. He has a privileged and even somewhat elite pedigree, but he is willing to forget all of this. He has also acted in ways that were harmful to the cause of Christ, but he is willing to let this go as well. The past, with its blessings and curses, its successes and failures, can become a distraction to the singular calling that is God's plan and purpose for him. In reading various letters written by Paul, we do sense his attempt to come to grips with his past: He recounts his conversion and call, his mystical experiences, his political disagreements, his struggles with envy and rivalry, even his "thorn in my body" (2 Corinthians 12:7). Paul was haunted by the past, and perhaps he knew the hold it had on him. The past, it seems, is an obstacle to an urgent passion: Paul wants to "grab hold" of the goal, just as Christ has grabbed hold of him (Philippians 3:12)! And thus Paul will need to let go of something, that which lies behind him, in order to be free to move more fully into the future.

This is a challenge for us as well. We carry the weight of some anger, some resentment, some prejudice, or some source of pride or privilege. So often, we are even unaware of the weights that we carry or the extent to which they hold us back. In the season of Lent, we are called to self-examination and simplicity in order that we may discern the path that Jesus has taken. As we pray and turn our hearts inward, we uncover burdens and find the courage to let them go. As long as we carry unnecessary baggage, we will never experience the freedom that is God's gift to us (Galatians 5). But in letting go, we are set free to walk into newness of life.

Single-Minded Focus

In developing a new habit or way of life, one often develops a singular focus or a driving passion: to be free of debt, to lose weight, or to graduate from college. Disciplined persons then change their behaviors in order to arrive at these destinations. We find that shopping as a recreational activity loses its appeal. We think twice before eating when we are not actually hungry. Our walking, and then running, becomes a more common part of our daily routine. We inquire about ways to access education, beginning where we are. Some dream, some calling, places this focus at the center of our lives. We want to be free of the anxiety of financial debt; we recognize the danger of unhealthy patterns of eating and exercising; we yearn for learning that will create opportunities in life and work. The dream or calling, in time, begins to define us, and we become more focused people.

The apostle Paul speaks clearly of his focus: "I do this one thing" (Philippians 3:13). He is aware that he has not arrived. His life has the qualities of movement, humility, and self-examination. And so he is singularly driven toward a particular outcome. This single-minded pursuit can be found in traditions of Scripture, particularly in the Psalms:

> "The truly happy person
>> doesn't follow wicked advice,
>> doesn't stand on the road of sinners,
>> and doesn't sit with the disrespectful.
>
> Instead of doing those things,
>> these persons love the Lord's Instruction,
>> and they recite God's Instruction day and night!
>
> They are like a tree replanted by streams of water,
>> which bears fruit at just the right time
>> and whose leaves don't fade.
>> Whatever they do succeeds." (Psalm 1:1-3)

The singular focus of the psalmist is to meditate on the Lord's instruction. The outcome is likened to tree planted by streams of living waters, which yield an abundant harvest. In Paul's own life, and in his instruction to the Philippians, the ultimate goal is a deeper relationship with Jesus Christ, in his life, suffering, death, and Resurrection. And such a focused life produces a community that bears the fruit of humility, service, adoration, and fellowship (koinonia). The fruit comes from the single-mindedness of spiritual practice: a wholehearted devotion to Jesus Christ, who is Savior and Lord. To confess Jesus Christ as Savior is to relinquish the drive to justify ourselves in our own goodness or righteousness. To confess Jesus Christ as Lord is to place our lives in submission to him and to follow his example.

To be sure, these are confessions that we make along the way, but they are also ones that we renew in every season of life. We do not point back to a moment in time when we made a decision to embark on the Christian life, without a thought about the implications of that turning point for each successive movement in our journeys. Because we are tempted to trust in our own righteousness, to deny our own sinfulness and to seek our own power, we have a constant need to renew our faith. In reciting his own spiritual struggle, Paul encourages the Philippians, and us, to do the same.

Finally, we persevere in order to reach a destination: in Paul's language, "the prize of God's upward call in Christ Jesus" (Philippians 3:14). More than one biblical scholar has asked the obvious question: "What is the prize?" The answer is not easily discovered. One has to consider the corpus of Paul's writings to the first generations of those who followed Jesus to approach some semblance of a response.

We will be helped in our search by locating the importance of "call" in Paul's life. He is clearly called from one way of life to another, from persecutor to evangelist, from skeptic to believer. His call experience, narrated in Acts 9, includes both the call to confess Jesus as Savior and Lord and the call to ministry. As Fred Craddock notes in his commentary on Philippians, these are not separate experiences in Paul's journey. The call is clear, convincing, and unmistakable. Of course Paul's call is not the template for every Christian's life; note how different is the call to Timothy, which Paul describes in 2 Timothy 1. Timothy's call was a formative experience that came developmentally through his grandmother and his mother (2 Timothy 1:5-7). Some who read this study will have had a dramatic experience of call, similar to Paul; others will have known a more natural exposure to the faith, as with Timothy.

Regardless, it is the call of God that leads us toward the prize, the end, the destination. "Our citizenship is in heaven," Paul writes (Philippians 3:20). It is heaven to which he is called, along with the Philippians and us. The "upward call" reminds us of the repetitive language of descending and ascending in Philippians: Paul wants to be in heaven, with the Lord, and yet he is motivated also to be present with his friends at Philippi (1:21-24). Jesus empties himself and takes the form of a servant, but God has highly exalted him (2:6-11). The upward call is experienced paradoxically through a life of obedience to God and humility toward one another. The fullness of this "upward call" is surely one that includes both this life and the life to come: We know Christ in the present moment, and yet we confess, in the words of the apostle's profound meditation on love (1 Corinthians 13), that now we know only in part. Then, when we have finally reached the prize for which we strive—

when are in the presence of God—we shall know, even as we are fully known.

Questions for Reflection and Discussion

1. What negative habit(s) you would like to eliminate? Or, what positive habit(s) you would like to undertake? How might you focus your efforts toward these goals?
2. To what extent are prayer and other spiritual practices a habit for you? What benefits do you see in habitual spiritual discipline?
3. Do you know someone who exhibits the qualities of transparency and authenticity? How do these qualities affect their relationships and sense of self?
4. Can you recall a time when you felt "stuck" in your spiritual life? How were you able to move forward?
5. Describe an area of your life where you currently feel "stuck" or stalled in a kind of "status quo." What changes can you make to move forward now?
6. What does God want you to leave in the past in order that you might be freed for faithful living in the present and future?
7. What can you do in your prayer life to continue straining forward toward Christ?

Prayer

O God,
grant me the humility
to recognize my flaws and failures
but also the confidence to trust in your power
that makes all things new;

through Jesus Christ,
who lives and reigns with you and the Holy Spirit,
One God, now and forever. Amen.

Focus for the Week

Make a list of three changes you would like to see in your own spiritual practices. One might be an activity you wish to give up or stop; a second might be a renewed time of prayer or study; and a third might be intentional time strengthening a relationship. Can you commit to a period of one month to see these changes emerge? After you make your list, reflect on it each day in prayer this week. Ask God to help you discern the particular shape of God's upward call in your life and to help you persevere as you strive toward it.

Prayer and Discipleship

Scripture: Read Philippians 3:17–4:9

"Practice these things: whatever you learned, received, heard, or saw in us" (Philippians 4:9).

C hristianity is a way of life. Before it is a system of beliefs or ideas, it is a way of life. This way is modeled on the life, suffering, death, and resurrection of Jesus Christ. When he encounters the first disciples, he calls them to follow him. He teaches them, but it is clear that the disciples find him compelling because his teaching resonates with the way he lives. As Matthew notes in the Sermon on the Mount, Jesus taught them as "someone with authority" (7:29), and his authority was grounded in the integrity of his example.

Christianity flourishes when there are visible models of Christ-like witness. This witness is not necessarily characterized by intellectual brilliance and precision, although clarity of thinking and believing is helpful in teaching the faith. More crucially, this witness is the truthful reminder of the life of Jesus, upon which his teaching was based. Jesus taught about the bread of life as he fed the hungry.

Jesus called the disciples to serve as he washed their feet. Jesus spoke of the light coming into the world as he gave sight to the blind. Jesus insisted that a physician came not to the well, but to the sick as he healed and touched the unclean.

In a modern world, a compelling witness was often associated with a rational explanation (or apologetic) about the Christian faith, an intellectual argument that could lead a person to explore all of the options. In the end, a modernist witness would insist that Jesus was the way, the truth, and the life via the intellectual persuasion of the speaker or writer. Two of the most significant examples of such a modern witness to the faith were C. S. Lewis's *Mere Christianity* and Josh McDowell's *Evidence That Demands a Verdict*.

The challenge for us in the twenty-first century is that we no longer live in the modern world; at least in Western culture, we live now in a postmodern world. And witness in a postmodern world is compelling not for its intellectual brilliance or clarity—we cannot reason or argue others into the faith—but for its visibility and coherence. Integrity is more relevant in a postmodern world than clarity.

The good news is that the twenty-first century shares many parallels with the first century. The witness of Jesus, and Paul after him, was closely bound up with the lives that they led. Jesus drew disciples into his circle of influence and told them he had given them an example, to love one another. In the next generation, the apostle Paul is bold enough to say to the Philippians "become imitators of me" (Philippians 3:17).

Become Imitators of Me

Discipleship is imitation. We are apprentices of Jesus who watch him teach, work, heal, forgive, and pray. As we watch and imitate him doing these things, we learn how to do them ourselves. We see his example in the apostle Paul, who would also teach, work, heal, forgive, pray, and bear witness to the living Lord. And we give thanks, in every generation, for those who seek daily to take up the cross and follow Jesus.

One of the contexts of the Letter to the Philippians is a conflict that is playing out in the congregation. In the early verses of Chapter 4, Paul identifies the specifics of the situation:

> I urge Euodia and I urge Syntyche to come to an agreement in the Lord. Yes, and I'm also asking you, loyal friend, to help these women who have struggled together with me in the ministry of the gospel, along with Clement and the rest of my coworkers whose names are in the scroll of life. (Philippians 4:2-3)

He identifies the people involved and offers a plan of action. But note that Paul does not go first to blame and scapegoating; instead, he urges the two women (Euodia and Syntyche) to be of one mind, echoing the teaching to the entire community in 2:1-2.

How are we to be of the same mind in the midst of divisions and conflict? We have the same mind (attitude) that was in Christ Jesus, who emptied himself and went to the cross for us (Philippians 2:5-11). In our own time, to empty ourselves might imply giving up advantage and setting aside pride. Jesus relinquishes equality with God, emptying himself for humanity in order that we might be reconciled to God. It was an advantage, an identity that properly belonged to him, and yet he was willing to set it aside for the sake of love. How might we be called to do the same, adopting the attitude of Christ Jesus in our own circumstances? I remember the wisdom of a friend, whose challenge to me, in the midst of a deep church conflict, took the form of a question: "Would we rather be right, or would we rather be in a right relationship?"

In some instances, reconciliation is needed before growth in the Christian community can be possible. Certainly, experiences of betrayal, abuse, and hypocrisy become obstacles to a world that does not see Jesus Christ clearly; instead they see the actions of his followers as departures from the love and grace of God. In these instances the need for reconciliation—including repentance, forgiveness, and restoration—can almost present itself as a demonstration of the removal of unclean spirits from the body.

Yet it is also true that reconciliation is a fundamental and necessary practice of what it means to be a disciple of Jesus Christ. Because Jesus offered the forgiveness of sins and reconciled humanity to God, we also proclaim the possibility of forgiveness and reconciliation among ourselves. Paul cannot avoid the reality of conflict between church leaders, even as he writes in thanksgiving for a gift. He must address the conflict if he is to teach the wholeness of the gospel.

The church today finds itself enmeshed in deep divisions. Some of the divisions are related to past harms, some to injustices in the present. In some expressions of the global church, the divisions are found along ethnic lines. In some denominations, the divisions are the result of disagreement around matters related to human sexuality. In some communities, the divisions arise around tragic events related to racial violence. And in some congregations, the divisions stem from betrayal by leaders or differences around worship and priorities.

We follow the examples of Jesus and Paul when we move toward the conflict rather than avoiding it. We imitate them in believing that the cross is God's ultimate sign of reconciliation, forgiveness, and restoration. We are not naive about the difficulty at the heart of the ministry of reconciliation, or the personal and human cost involved. In the days of Holy Week, Jesus moves toward the cross and dies there for us; the apostle Paul would later write to the Galatians, "I bear the marks of Jesus on my body" (Galatians 6:17). In the same way, as we imitate Jesus in the ministry of reconciliation we know we can expect a painful struggle.

And so, Paul writes, practice what you saw in us, as he speaks the truth in love to a divided church and calls them to a more excellent way.

"Be Glad in the Lord Always!"

Joy, or gladness, is a prominent theme in Philippians. The Greek words for joy or rejoice occur fourteen times in this brief letter. The persistence of joy is somewhat remarkable, given the circumstances: Paul writes from a prison cell, and there are realities within the church that disturb him, including envy and rivalry among preachers of the gospel (can you imagine?)! There is even a specific directive to two individuals to get along, to "come to an agreement in the Lord" (Philippians 4:2). The deadly sin of pride and the human experience of conflict, it seems, were present in the earliest churches. Even more remarkable is the fact that the Philippian church was one of the healthier congregations in the first century, compared to the church at Corinth, for example, which was in chaos. A particular sign of the Philippians' health was a gift they had sent to Paul, and the primary occasion of the letter was to say thank you. And yet even they were not above rivalry and conflict.

Amidst all of this, Paul rejoices and commands his readers, and us, to rejoice. "Be glad in the Lord always! Again I say, be glad!" (Philippians 4:4). If you read Philippians closely, the focus on joy emerges despite situations that are anything but joyful. Paul emphasizes joy in the face of impending death (Chapter 1); joy in the midst of suffering (Chapter 2); joy in the experience of sacrifice and letting go (Chapter 3); and joy quite apart from external conditions (Chapter 4). "I know the experience of being in need and of having more than enough," Paul writes. He has been full and hungry, has had plenty and been poor (Philippians 4:12). And yet he says, rejoice.

Karl Barth, the great theologian of the last century, regarded joy in Philippians as the defiant "nevertheless" that counters all the negative circumstances of the Christian life. One of my favorite cartoons has two monks seated together, dressed in their habits. One says to the other, "Apart from piles, varicose veins, a hernia, and leprosy, God has been very good to me." Despite his sorrows, he recognizes what God has done and finds reason to rejoice. Joy in Philippians, joy in the Christian life, is often a defiant "nevertheless." This gladness, Paul insists, is "in the Lord," who is near (Philippians 4:4-5). In the Christian calendar, the church has placed this passage for reading in the season of Advent and also late in the season of Pentecost. We thus recognize two meanings in Paul's words: The Lord is near in anticipation of his birth, and the Lord is near in the promised gift of the comforter, the encourager, the Holy Spirit.

So how do we adopt Paul's command to be glad always? We begin by making the distinction between gladness, or joy, and happiness. Happiness is a human pursuit; joy is a divine gift. Joy is a deeper reality than happiness, and less tied to external circumstances. Thus Paul can rejoice, even in prison. Is Paul happy? Most likely not. Is he joyful? Yes.

The intention to rejoice always is to be attentive to the coming of the Lord in every season and circumstance. I do not believe that God is the author of the great challenges that come to us.

But I do believe God is present within them—incarnate in his Son, Jesus Christ, and dwelling in us through the power of the Holy Spirit. In some of the economically desperate villages on this earth, where life and death are a daily matter of prayer and lament, I have witnessed women and men who courageously echo the defiant words of the apostle Paul: Be glad in the Lord always. The Lord is near.

Don't Be Anxious

Disciples imitate Jesus. They are reconcilers. They are glad in all circumstances. And disciples are taught not to be anxious. As Paul writes, "Don't be anxious about anything; rather, bring up all of your requests to God in your prayers and petitions, along with giving thanks" (Philippians 4:6). Here Paul reflects on the destructiveness of anxiety, a word that is relevant to most every one of us. This echoes a teaching of Jesus in the Sermon on the Mount: "Don't worry about your life . . . " (Matthew 6:25). What is anxiety? For many it is the free-floating sense that conditions are beyond our comprehension, and we are not in control. Sources of anxiety might be our family of origin, the uncertainty of our financial circumstances, or fears about what is happening or might happen in the lives of our children or parents. Anxiety is real.

Some would argue that anxiety is increasingly harmful. Thanks to technology, the United States has become a chronically anxious nation. Think of cable news, financial news, social media, medical and terror alerts. Constant access to up-to-the-minute information fuels our anxious fires, giving us reason to worry every time we turn on the television or check our phones. There is a low-level but almost universal chronic anxiety, and to breathe the air in our culture is to experience it.

So what does Scripture teach us—have no anxiety about anything? I don't think Paul is urging us to live in denial, to bury our heads in the sand. He is certainly not suggesting that we ignore the needs of others, which would display a lack of compassion. Again, Paul is reflecting on the destructive power of anxiety, where we become paralyzed and overwhelmed. But Paul reminds us that we can respond in another way. While we are powerless to control the external realities that surround us, we can respond as disciples with a spiritual practice. Paul commands us to "bring up all of your requests to God in your prayers and petitions, along with giving thanks" (Philippians 4:6).

We establish a connection. We are silent before God; we speak honestly with God about what we need; we give thanks to God. This is the spiritual life, the inner life—silence, petition, and gratitude. What is my greatest need? I can only answer this question when I have spent time in reflection. For what am I grateful? I can only answer this question when I have engaged in contemplation. To ask God is to believe in an unseen power who provides in the future. To give thanks to God is to trust in an unseen power who has provided in the past. At times we take on too much responsibility—we over function—and this exhibits a practical atheism. Are we anxious because we're living as though it's all up to us? Do we actually believe in a God who is real, trust in a God who intervenes?

In this brief passage from Philippians there is a progression. How do we move from anxiety to peace? In the words of the hymn, we "take it to the Lord in prayer." This is not a quick fix, but a lifelong process. In our spiritual formation, and in our journey as disciples, we claim the promise of Philippians 1:6 that the God who started a good work in us will be faithful to complete it. All of this is a gift from God, yet it also requires our participation.

In offering our prayers and petitions to God, we are given yet an additional promise: "The peace of God that exceeds all understanding will keep your hearts and minds safe in Christ Jesus" (Philippians 4:7). Another translation, instead of "keep safe," says that God's peace will "guard" our hearts and minds (NRSV). Paul intentionally chooses a military word here. God, through the gift of peace, will *guard* our hearts and minds. We imagine the apostle, in a prison cell, being watched by a guard, and in his own mind seeing this as a parable. In the same way that faith allows us to withstand pressures that are external to us, it gives us a peace that secures us.

To experience the peace that exceeds all understanding is to know that hope is more than optimism, peace is more than getting along, and joy is deeper than happiness. Indeed, hope may be present in despair, peace in conflict, and joy amidst great suffering. The persistence of a defiant joy bears witness to the power of the gospel, which is finally the path of the disciple from anxiety to peace. At a practical level, this is our capacity to remain connected to one another and to God. We are connected to a worshiping community that sends a different message than the chronically anxious chorus of our culture; we are connected to a body of Christ that, at its best, is a community of grace and forgiveness. But more deeply we are also and ultimately connected to the One who is always with us and for us—Jesus, who is himself the peace of God that surpasses all understanding.

Focus Your Thoughts on These Things

Finally, discipleship is about the life of the mind. Paul writes: "From now on, brothers and sisters, if anything is excellent and if anything is admirable, focus your thoughts on these things: all that is true, all that is holy, all that is just, all that is pure, all that is lovely, and all that is worthy of praise" (4:8). If imitation is practical application and rejoicing is doxology, focusing our thoughts is attending to the intellectual life. It is, in the language of Jesus, loving God with all our minds (see Matthew 22:37). The apostle calls us to turn our intellect toward that which is true, holy, just, pure, and lovely.

Paul offers a list here of virtues that the Greek philosophers also recognized and upheld. Here a Christian is given yet again a model. It is true that we are often prone to set ourselves against and apart from the political and moral discourse of our culture. We do want to retain the distinctiveness of the Christian witness. And yet Paul the evangelist and missionary sought a way to build a bridge to the culture. He found a common ground between the ideals of Christian life and the virtues of the world in which he lived. Might we find such common ground today? Fred Craddock speaks of the experience we often have of observing men and women who do not live by faith and yet lead lives of great character. If we follow Paul's instructions to the Philippians, we will recognize and praise their uprightness rather than see them as rivals.

And so a Lenten discipline might simply be to seek the good, the true, and the beautiful wherever we find it in this world, and to praise God for these gifts. Instead of first looking for fault and failure, we might focus our thoughts on all that is worthy of praise. As we do this, we become aware that God is present in the world through prevenient or common grace. We train our imaginations to recognize virtue, justice, grace, and reconciliation wherever we find these qualities: in novels and films, in political leaders, and in ordinary workplaces.

I confess that this is not my default response in everyday life. I am often quick to judge. I have been trained to observe with suspicion and to question the purity of motives and intentions. There is sometimes a place for this—God does not call us to be naive. And yet God is calling us to a transformed life of the mind, where we focus our thoughts on all that is holy and just, true and pure, lovely and worthy of praise. When we do so, we will receive a vision that is at the heart of all things: We will discover that we have been focusing our thoughts on the cross of Jesus Christ.

Questions for Reflection and Discussion

1. Can you think of a person in your own experience whose life you have sought to imitate? Why did you select this person?
2. Where in your life are you imitating Christ? How might others look to you as an example worthy of imitation?
3. What song, hymn, or chorus takes you to a place of rejoicing?
4. What relationship do you see between prayer and joy? How can you strengthen this relationship in your own life?
5. Is there a particular spiritual practice that helps you to overcome anxiety?
6. Where have you witnessed truth, beauty, or goodness in the lives of persons of no faith or other faiths?
7. How might we in the church build bridges toward these persons?

Prayer

O God,
we thank you for a way of life
that has been shown to us in Jesus Christ.
Help us to be imitators of him.
Move us to be agents of reconciliation.
Guide us to rejoice in all things.
And grant us your peace. Amen.

Focus for the Week

As you reflect on the life of Jesus and the community at Philippi, imagine practical ways that you might imitate the way of life being taught by Paul. As you pray this week, find an occasion to be glad; discover God's peace in the midst of anxiety; and move toward persons in conflict with the confidence that reconciliation is possible. Ask God to speak through you and to use you in these situations.

Prayer and Gratitude

Scripture: Read Philippians 4:10-23

"*My God will meet your every need . . .*" *(Philippians 4:19).*

I n the fourth chapter of Philippians, the apostle Paul relates how he has come to grips with the circumstances of his life.

"*I have learned how to be content in any circumstance*" *(4:11).*

"*I can endure all these things through the power of the one who gives me strength*" *(4:13).*

"*My God will meet your every need out of his riches in the glory that is found in Christ Jesus*" *(4:19).*

Paul's honesty here is helpful to us in our own journey: Faith can be a source of strength for those who encounter the ups and downs of life. In good circumstances and in bad, Paul expresses confidence in Christ and experiences solace in him. The late Fred

Craddock, a wonderful teacher of preachers and interpreter of Scripture, comments on the *whether-or-not* nature of the gospel: Paul trusts in the gospel's power whether he is present with the Philippians or absent; whether he is alive or dead; whether he experiences hunger or fullness; whether he lives in scarcity or abundance; whether he is in prison or free.[1]

Bad News, Good News, Who Knows?

A simple but powerful lesson for us in this passage is that Paul is not defined by the circumstances of his life. I am reminded of an ancient Chinese story about a man who owned a horse. One day, the horse ran away. The man's friend said, "So sorry about your horse." The man replied, "Bad news, good news, who knows?" A few days later the horse came back with a herd of wild horses. The man's friend said, "Wonderful!" The man said, "Good news, bad news, who knows?" The next day one of the wild horses threw the man's son and broke both of the son's legs. "How awful," said the friend. "Bad news, good news, who knows?" said the man. Later all of young men in the village were called into war, but the son with the broken legs was excused. Good news, bad news, who knows?

I hear echoes of Paul in this story. He refuses to be defined by the circumstances in which he finds himself. In fact, he has a kind of holy indifference as he writes to the Philippians: "I have learned the secret to being content in any and every circumstance, whether full or hungry or whether having plenty or being poor" (4:12). Paul knows who he is, and he does not allow himself to be limited or overcome by externals. Fred Craddock comments again:

"[Paul] is able to live with abundance, but it is not necessary that he have it. He is able to live in hunger and want, but it is not necessary that he be poor. He is defined neither by wealth nor poverty but by a contentment that transcends both and by a power in Christ which enables him to live in any circumstance."[2]

I am convinced that this is the word of the Lord for many of Christ's followers today. Too often we are defined, overcome, overwhelmed, demoralized, impressed, awed, or otherwise shaped by external circumstances. Yet it matters more what goes on inside of us. Could it be that what happens around us is not as important as what happens within us?

Paul is in prison as he writes the letter to the Philippians, yet he refuses to see himself as a victim. Rather, one senses throughout his letter that he sees himself as a person who is empowered by God regardless of his situation. It is easy to allow the world to pin us down, to determine who we are, and to set the agenda for us. How do we get beyond this? The answer we see in Paul is, we work on our own spiritual lives. We look within; we claim a radical faith in the God who is trustworthy, and we rely on the One who will provide all the resources we need to live each day.

There is a wonderful story told by a rabbi: "When I started I wanted to save the whole world. I lived a little longer, and thought, maybe I will just save my nation. Then I lived a little longer and thought, maybe I will just save my city. Then I lived a little longer and thought, maybe I'll just save my family. When I became an old man, and had lived a long while, I realized, maybe I'll just save myself! And then it dawned on me: If I had tried to save myself first, then maybe I could save my family, and my city, and my nation, and my world!"

We work on our own spiritual lives. If we want other people to serve, we serve. If we want other people to be more generous, we ourselves become more generous. If we want other people to be less judgmental, we commit to judging others less. If we want other people to be more faithful, we strive to live more faithfully ourselves. Because Paul is working on his own relationship with God, he is able to change himself, his community, and ultimately his world. It begins with us, within us. We do not allow the world to define us. "Don't be conformed to patterns of this world," Paul writes in Romans 12:2, "but be transformed by the renewing of your minds."

Our Spiritual Lives

What is involved in working on our own spiritual lives? This is an essential question if we are going to mature in the journey of following Jesus, which is also the way of life that keeps us near the cross. One answer we have identified in this study is prayer. Prayer is an essential part of the ongoing Lenten disciplines of self-examination, repentance, and taking responsibility for our own spiritual lives. As we talk to God, and listen for God's words to us, we recognize that our self-worth is not defined by externals: our houses, toys, degrees, perks, jobs, achievements, setbacks, or obstacles. Remember Paul's profound reflection on his self-worth and identity at the beginning of Philippians 3. He had everything going for him and willingly counted it as a loss because he found his identity in Christ. Paul is the model for us, and indeed, he continually calls us to imitate him. So how do we imitate the apostle's example, separated in time from him by two thousand years?

Paul's teaching and example may be more relevant and challenging to us than we might first imagine. Someone once observed that "we buy things we do not need with money we do not have to impress people we do not know!" We wittingly or unwittingly ground our self-worth in things, or the money to purchase those things, or the opinions of those we wish to impress. But such things are not what ultimately determine our value, though many would have us believe it. What is the true source of our self-worth? Our self-worth is rooted in the grace of God. We depend on the grace of God to complete what we cannot do in ourselves. We trust God to provide for our needs. And once we know this, we can live less anxious, more contented lives. Paul reminds us: "Don't be anxious about anything; rather, bring up all of your requests to God in your prayers and petitions, along with giving thanks. Then the peace of God that exceeds all understanding will keep your hearts and minds safe in Christ Jesus" (Philippians 4:6-7).

God's Provision

The Letter to the Philippians is an extended and intimate communication between a Christian leader and a community that he knows well. Along the way, he reflects on a variety of subjects, some more theological and even mystical, others more autobiographical and relational. And yet by the conclusion of the letter, Paul has circled back to his original purpose: He is writing to thank them for their very tangible partnership (koinonia) in the gospel (1:5), which has come in the form of a financial gift. He writes at the end of Chapter 4 about their support of his ministry, expressing deep gratitude for the gifts the Philippians have sent (4:10-20).

For almost three decades, I served as a pastor in the local church. This work included a number of recurring experiences: baptisms and weddings, confirmation classes and professions of faith, committee meetings and resolution of conflicts, observances of Advent and Lent, and celebrations of Christmas and Easter. And across those years there was an additional act of ministry that was a constant presence: the need to discover the financial resources to sustain the work of those local churches.

I have been in conversation with more than one pastor friend who has shared with me that this is his or her least favorite aspect of ministry. I would add that a number of laity friends have said to me, "I will do anything in the church except ask people for money!" Clergy and lay members alike, it seems, would rather avoid raising money. It's regarded as a necessary task, but not a desirable one.

Over time, however, circumstances led me to a different perspective. In a wonderful kind of way, coming to the ministry of stewardship each year drove me back to the basics: trusting that God would provide. It was an occasion for me to give thanks, on behalf of the congregation, for the provision of our financial needs. It was a yearly reminder that we are not defined by external circumstances: My self-worth (as a leader) and our value as a congregation was rooted in God's grace.

I have found extraordinary wisdom in the way the apostle Paul communicates with the Philippians on this subject. He affirms his contentment, describes the power that comes from it, and then expresses trust in the future. Such is the power of gratitude.

Paul begins with an affirmation: "I have learned how to be content in any circumstance" (4:11). One hears in these words the virtue of simplicity. Contentment is making peace with what we have rather than obsessing about what we do not yet possess. Contentment is focusing on who we are rather than comparing ourselves to others. There is in the word contentment a deep theological maturity: We honor who we are, as men and women created in God's image. When we are content we embrace our finite natures; we are creatures with boundaries, not the Creator with unlimited power and unrestrained expectations.

In verse 12, Paul affirms that he has learned the "secret" of contentment, suggesting that such knowledge is not obvious to the world.

We can readily observe this to be true. There is a profound lack of contentment, even in the most prosperous nation on the planet, and often among the most affluent of her inhabitants. I offer this observation not for the purpose of cynical judgment, because many of us are complicit in cultures of commerce and consumption that keep us from knowing contentment. Rather, I say this to highlight the benefits of learning the contentment that Paul enjoys. I have often been in conversation with friends who seemed to be guided by the assumption that certain future events—getting a promotion at work, the children finishing school, paying off a mortgage, getting out of debt, moving to a smaller city—would allow them to be more content. And indeed there may have been something to their reflections and hopes. Yet Paul speaks of a different reality: "I have learned how to be content in any circumstance." He has known abundance and scarcity; he has been hungry and he has feasted at the banquet table. Through faith and trust in God, he now knows that contentment comes from a different source. Contentment comes from God, and it resides within Paul rather than in his situation.

Because of this, Paul is empowered. He proclaims, "I can endure all these things through the power of the one who gives me strength" (Philippians 4:13). We might reflect on all that Paul is enduring as he pens these words: imprisonment; the questioning of his motives; rivalry among other evangelists; divisiveness in the church that he loves; and the possibility of his impending death. Even so, he is confident that he can endure all these things. This is a testament to his resilience.

In our spiritual journeys, we also seek ways to become more resilient. In my own life, I have been strengthened by relationships with Christian friends, participation in the church's worship and fellowship, engagement in spiritual disciplines, and guidance from a spiritual director. The phrase "I can endure all these things" can be a deceptive statement, giving the impression that we are independent. In reality, Paul always leads and serves alongside friends and coworkers in the faith. These bonds help Paul to be more resilient; his meditation on the body of Christ in 1 Corinthians 12–14 reminds us that we are not primarily individual spiritual beings. Instead, we are members of a body, strengthening and supporting one another.

This is the source of our resilience. The one who gives us strength is Jesus Christ, and this power often comes to us through the presence of his people. Paul is encouraged by the tangible gifts of the Philippians. He writes, "I now have plenty and it is more than enough. I am full to overflowing because I received the gifts that you sent from Epaphroditus. Those gifts give off a fragrant aroma, an acceptable sacrifice that pleases God"(4:18).

In the Old and New Testaments, the fragrant aroma of an offering often describes how it pleases God. The sacrifices acceptable to God shift from particular ritual acts to ones that express an internal motivation: In the words of the Psalmist, a spirit that his humble before God (Psalm 51). In 2 Corinthians 2:15, Paul writes of the church, "We smell like the aroma of Christ's offering to God, both to those who are being saved and to those who are on the road to destruction." In Ephesians 5:2, Paul writes that Christ loved us and gave himself for us as "a sacrificial offering that smelled sweet to God."

In Paul's Letter to the Philippians, the aroma of the gift signifies their love for him and his love for them. When Paul receives the gift from the Philippians, he understands it to be an offering given by people who are shaped by the cross. We draw near to the cross as we receive the gifts and blessings of God, and we draw near to the cross as we open our hearts and hands to give sacrificially. This is the intimate relation of giving and receiving that is at the heart of the triune God.

Paul concludes with a word of trust and confidence: "My God will meet your every need out of his riches in the glory that is found in Christ Jesus" (Philippians 4:19). In his own life he has experienced this gracious provision of God, and he now becomes a witness of this good news. This is a powerful testimony. The church today is blessed when echoes of this testimony are heard in our own lives. I have been the beneficiary of extraordinary gifts in life and ministry: family, teachers, coaches, mentors, experiences, and opportunities. At times I have wondered about the next steps, and frankly I have not seen a way forward. And yet, in the language of the spiritual, "God has made a way out of no way." Or in the language of Paul, God has met every need "out of his riches in the glory that is found in Christ Jesus."

I have experienced these gifts in tangible ways. And yet I also see the provision of God in its deeper meaning, particularly in the season of Lent as we journey toward a garden, a cross, and an empty tomb. God meets every need of ours, according to his riches in glory. We have a deep need for communion with God. Jesus, who enters into this world, gives himself for us. He literally empties himself for us, in order that we might be in a right relationship with God. This is the atonement, the complete and sufficient sacrifice. God is with us; indeed, God is for us, in Jesus Christ. And in his life and work, he meets every need of ours according to his riches in glory. This need includes abundance in the present and in the life to come. And this is the promise of Easter fulfilled in the gift of the risen Lord, who is always with us (Matthew 28:20).

There is deep fulfillment in becoming a disciple of Jesus Christ. This fulfillment does not shield us from uncertainty, complexity, or conflict. But this fulfillment is grounded in the power and goodness of God, which we see most clearly in the cross of Jesus Christ. We move nearer to the cross when we make or renew a commitment to follow him. We come into communion with him when we take up his cross daily. And we make his presence more visible in the world when we share in his mission: to redeem humanity, to restore persons into a right relationship with God and one another, and to recreate persons in his image, which is love.

This recreation is the journey from death to life, from Ash Wednesday to Easter Sunday and beyond. We give all praise and glory to God for this work in us, and we draw strength from the words of the apostle Paul: "The one who started a good work in you will stay with you to complete the job" (Philippians 1:6).

Questions for Reflection and Discussion

1. Can you recall a time when your life was in a state of complexity and challenge, and yet you knew the contentment of which Paul speaks?
2. Can you remember the experience of receiving a significant gift from a friend? What did this mean to you?
3. How has life taught you to be resilient?
4. Has your church passed through a significant challenge that made the community stronger?
5. Can you recall an experience where God met your needs?

Prayer

O God, we trust you.

Through it all, we have known your provisions.

Teach us to be content in any and all circumstances.

In the name and spirit of Jesus Christ who loved us and gave himself for us. Amen.

Focus for the Week

As you pray this week, reflect on your basic needs. How has God met them? Pray with a posture of gratitude, thanking God for providing. Then reflect on your generosity toward others. As you pray, focus on how God is leading you to simplify your life; how you can be more generous; and how you can meet the needs of someone who is experiencing a crisis.

An Additional Focus

Take ten minutes to reflect on a cross that is visually before you. How have you experienced the love of God? And how is God's love being channeled through you toward others? Conclude with a prayer of thanksgiving.

1. From *Philippians*, by Fred Craddock (John Knox, 1985); page 77.
2. From *Philippians*, by Fred Craddock (John Knox, 1985); page 78.